# Folk Tales
# of
# Thailand

## P.C. Roy Chaudhury

*Illustrated by*
*Susan Harmer*

## M
## MACMILLAN
## PUBLISHERS

First published 1976 by Sterling Publishers Pvt, Ltd, India
This edition published 1990, under licence from
Sterling Publishers.

Published by *Macmillan Publishers Ltd*
London and Basingstoke
*Associated companies and representatives in Accra,*
*Auckland, Delhi, Dublin, Gaborone, Hamburg, Harare,*
*Hong Kong, Kuala Lumpur, Lagos, Manzini, Melbourne,*
*Mexico City, Nairobi, New York, Singapore, Tokyo*

ISBN 0 – 333 – 53207 – 4

Printed in Singapore

A CIP catalogue record for this book is available from the British Library.

# Contents

# Introduction

The folk tales of a country are a vital element in its living culture and reflect an image of its people. While in Thailand in 1974 I studied the country and its people and was particularly interested in the Thai folk tales as an aid.

Before making a study of the folklore of a country one should get to know the broad outlines of the land and the people. This is what I did. A number of Thai friends were very kind and the excellent library of the Siam Society in Bangkok was useful. Before discussing the Thai folk tales, it is necessary, therefore, to describe Thailand.

Originally known as Siam, Thailand is in the centre of the Indo-Chinese peninsular and covers an area about as large as France (about 200,000 square miles). A long splinter running from the central mass down to Malaya gives it a distinctive shape described as an elephant's head with a protruding trunk.

The country is split into 71 provinces and each province into several districts. It has a border with Burma, Laos, Cambodia and Malaysia and has been very closely related to India in terms of religion, trade and culture.

There is a variety of ethnic groups of which the Thais are dominant, distributed over four distinct geograhic zones.

Industrially, Thailand is poor, although the extraction of teak wood, gems, tin, gum and other forest products helps to maintain a fairly comfortable standard of living for the population of about 55 million.

The country is not over populated but the World Health Organisation is wisely phasing in a birth control programme so that the problems of population explosion facing other countries like India do not trouble Thailand.

Bangkok, the capital is a heavily populated modern city which dominates most aspects of life in Thailand. It became known as the Venice of the East because there used to be *klongs* (canals) running parallel to many roads. Now some of them are being filled in and used as roads too.

The language of the country is Thai. Family names have come into use only in the course of the last 50 or 60 years according to the decree of the King that every family must have a name.

Primary education is compulsory and every primary school pupil has to come to school in uniform. Education is free up to a certain level but for higher education Thais are more keen to go to America and Europe.

Government service is the aim of educated boys and girls but the government is not the largest employer. Most urban Thais are self-employed. A fair percentage work in the hotels and eating places and the rivers offer employment to quite a few.

There are many corporate or cooperative organisations in Thailand, but the Thais do not save money for the sake of saving. If they do save anything they like to use it to travel, to see new places or revisit old places until the money runs out. They love giving presents too. The menfolk love to laze about sometimes, gambling and amusing themselves. They are not attracted by the monetary rewards of working overtime.

The hundreds of hotels and eating places are mainly meant for tourists but the Thais also patronise them liberally. Tourism has certainly added another dimension to the Thai way of life.

The traditional foods of Thailand are rice, noodles, fish, chicken and pork. Milk is not consumed much whereas vegetables and herbs are commonly eaten. Thai food in general is very tasty.

Politically, Thailand has never been the colony of a larger power but it has been under the strong influence of several other powers at the same time. France and England have been prominent at one time or another. The Americans came later. India, Burma and China had, and still have, strong cultural and trade relations with China.

The Thais are excellent diplomats and appear to have often played off one power against another. In 1821, a military doctor called Dr Crawfurd was sent to Siam by the Governor-General of India to obtain trade concessions from the King. The King stood on his dignity and did not allow him any latitude as he was the agent of the King-Emperor of Great Britain. Crawfurd also failed because he went out of his depths and dabbled in some political research on the vulnerability of Siam and carried out some unauthorised surveys. The Crawfurd papers published in the National Library in Bangkok in recent years are an interesting study of failure in diplomacy on Crawfurd's part.

The kingship in Thailand has many facets. After the political revolution of 1932, Thailand fell into the hands of the military core which ruled until 1973 when another movement ended militarism. Although the King has been shorn of many political powers, he is deeply venerated, loved and held sacred. The picture of the King and Queen can be seen everywhere.

The rural areas have but a fleeting interest in the political shifts that emanate from Bangkok. They know their village headman far better than the district officer; they know the abbot of the nearest monastery better than the police chief of the district.

The people are very attached to their country, with a strong sense of belonging; they are proud of Thailand, the Land of the Free. They are eclectic in outlook and would not allow a foreign wind to blow away their culture.

Despite being in close contact with China, Burma and India for so long, and with the United Kingdom and the United States more recently, they have retained all the nuances of Thai culture. Men and women of the elite have, by and large, adopted western dress but you still cannot enter the King's palace to sightsee without being properly dressed: men must wear ties.

The Thais are extremely courteous, helpful and polite and rather sophisticated. A Thai woman will bow gracefully when offering food and drink to a guest at her house. No one should enter the living area of the house with their shoes on.

It is a common maxim in Thailand that there is plenty of rice in the fields, plenty of fish in the water and the King is good — so why worry? The Thais are contented, cheerful, hospitable and open-hearted, but also sensitive to a social slight.

The people are neatly dressed and clean. They love flowers and Thai orchids are famous.

Undoubtedly, the keystone of Thai culture is religion. Some 90 per cent of the people are Buddhists, Theravada Buddhism being the traditional religion, in synthesis with Hinduism and Animism.

The original home of the Thais was in southern China. They came into contact with the Hindu civilisation through missionaries and, later, Buddhism penetrated from India to Ceylon and Burma. Siam had accepted Hinduism before Buddhism; the Brahmin priest is still revered and many court functions are still performed by both Hindu and Buddhist priests.

There are thousands and thousands of Buddhist *wats* or temples in the country and a similar number of images of Lord Buddha. The Emerald Buddha, the most venerated image of Buddha in the country, is said to have been brought from Patna in India. The monasteries have thousands of beautifully made images of Buddha in stone and bronze and many of the temples have wonderful murals.

There are also some very old Hindu temples, such as the one at Lopburi, with images of Hindu gods such as Brahma, Indra and so on. But there are also Christian and Muslim places of worship too.

Despite being intensely religious, the Thais have not made a fetish of Buddhism, rather they have made it enjoyable. They go to the temple in a spirit of respect mixed with gaiety but not levity. The temples and the *wats* are the focal point of their social activities.

During the holidays, you can see boys and girls studying their school and college books at the feet of the images of the Lord Buddha lined up by the wall. Some will have pulled up a chair and table from somewhere to study, others will be relaxing in the grounds or feeding the tortoises. Refreshments are available nearby.

The *wats* house the primary schools and some the higher standards schools too. Some of the monks are scholars, some are not. The lay Buddhists know this but do not venerate them less for it.

People take food and drink for the monks to celebrate birthdays. Cigarettes, soft drinks and so on, are offered to the monks and accepted and by offering the lay Buddhists are 'making merit' or acquiring virtue. By the ordination into monk-hood, even temporarily, the boy 'earns merit' for his parents. Some of the monks surprised me by saying they were going to the United States or to Australia to study the Business Management courses.

A young monk at Wat Arun told me he was a graduate in Philosophy of Benaras Hindu University and his next move was to get a Doctorate in Philosophy from the United States.

King Mongkut was the abbot of a big monastery in Bangkok for 27 years and was known to be a great scholar before he became the King.

The ruling religion of Buddhism has been made a very practical religion which one can follow and enjoy living in the family. The Buddhists are not vegetarians as most are in India.

The sight of the saffron-robed monks followed by one or two temple boys going round to collect alms in the morning is a familiar sight. The monks are not a liability to the country. They give back a lot in the form of running schools, teaching the Buddhist tenets and looking after the sick and giving medicines. The monks are allowed to visit houses although they shun women's company.

There is an active Department of Religious Affairs under the Education Ministry assisting the *wats* and the monks. The monks have to study and pass examinations up to the ninth grade or they may attend Buddhist monasteries. There are a number of foreign monks in Thailand. There is an organisation called the World Fellowship of Buddhists with headquarters in Bangkok which is a co-ordinating body.

The typical Thai family is basically self-sufficient and they live above the level of subsistence. They dress well and eat well. They do not as a rule, save. 'Making merit' is an item in the family budget.

The average Thai woman is contented and family orientated. They are not, by and large, feminists. Probably Buddhism has made the women soft and mellow. Educated Thai ladies now occupy good posts under the government in many disciplines. Petite, gay and somewhat westernised, educated Thai ladies love their homes and are gracious to guests and proud of their Thai culture.

Thai girls are brought up in a very natural way. Even in the rural areas a certain amount of wooing but no touching is permitted in front of parents. Marriages are expected to be registered. After marriage the couple starts a new home but this is not obligatory. Even in Bangkok there are rich and highly educated joint families with or without separate kitchens. Marriages are blessed by monks although they are solemnised by a civil ritual. Divorces are easy. An unmarried mother is readily accepted in the family. The society is not hard on the wronged girl.

With regard to funerals a dead body need not be cremated quickly. The body may be kept embalmed for months before cremation. Invitation to friends and relatives to witness the cremation is a social obligation.

The Thais have great respect for teachers, elders, monks and the royalty. This has probably led to a certain degree of self-acceptance and self-approval and carried to extremes it may be thwarting individual enterprise. However there is absolutely no casteism.

Two sports are much prized: kite-flying and Takrow. Takrow is the passing of a rattan ball in the air by a circle of men using their feet, shoulders and head but not their hands. Travel is another great recreation.

Sculpture and architecture are well-developed. There are a number of popular traditional Thai dance dramas. The musical instruments are mostly of Indian origin. Mural painting is well-developed.

From this picture of Thailand and the Thais we come on to a discussion of the folk tales. From happy and joy-loving people in a warm climate one could expect lively folk tales.

Thai folk tales have a lot of affinity with those of India. This is so because the Thais have kept up many Indian traditions which the Indians have lost or are losing. Thailand like India is based on an agricultural economy. Even now every agricultural operation is preceded by a ceremony. The official ploughing begins with the top official of the Agriculture Ministry ploughing in a symbolic manner. The *Hala-Karshan* ceremony when the first ploughing is done is preceded by *Bhumi-Puja* (worship of the land).

The seed scattering is also marked by a ceremony. When the crops ripen flags are put up suggesting that the rice-crop is pregnant and no one should disturb her.

If a house has to be built, a small spirit-house in the shape of a wooden temple is put up and offerings are made with joss-sticks and food. The idea is that by building a house you disturb a spirit. This is like the Hindu custom of worshipping the *basutu-devata* (the spirit of a particular home-stead).

One main source of the folk tales in Thailand is the Buddhist and Jain *Jataka* stories. The flora, fauna and birdlife of Thailand have naturally found their way into the folk tales particularly because of the *Jataka* stories. In the Jatakas we have stories about monkeys, dogs, oxen, peacocks, cranes, crabs, crows, pigeons, geese, fish, jackals, elephants, snakes, the mongoose, parrots, etc. These stories in their Thai versions have taken some local inflexion as could be expected.

Many of the folk tales of Thailand showing the wisdom of the Brahmins and the Buddhist monks, the hero's deeds, the fate of the over clever merchant, the fowler's archery, the King's generosity, the value of a friend or a brother are drawn from the *Jataka* stories.

The underlining of virtue, the exposure of evils or sin and the many moral tales in Thailand emanate from the elemental human feelings as in any other country. Some folk tales, like the elephant-catcher's tricks and follies, and the cheats in the garb of Buddhist monks are, however, of local origin.

The Ramayana of India known as the Ramakien in Thailand has a tremendous influence; it is the anchor of a main facet of Thai culture. Many of the folk tales, folk songs, rural paintings, cottage industries, plays and dramas, etc., are based on the Ramakien. I saw some excellent shadow plays and ballets based on Ramayana stories. Muslims are the main participants in many of the shadow-plays. Nang Yae, the Thai classical shadow-play has a very important role in retelling the stories in a captivating manner.

We find Ramakien stories in print on cloth and silk; they are known to every Thai child. Many folk tales are taken or based on Ramayana stories. The Thai Ramayana is not based on Valmiki's Ramayana but on the southern Tamil version of India.

Another source is the old and rich Siamese poetry. Prose-writing, essays and novels are more modern. But Siamese poetry is highly developed and ancient. Folk tales based on the poetry themes, entirely in verse have been handed down from generation to generation. Court poetry is another source of the folk tales.

The destruction of Ayuthya, once the capital of Siam destroyed a lot of literature but folk tales have a strange resilience; they survive through the granniers, pedlars, travellers, priests, tradesmen and the maritime folk.

But the greatest source of the folk tales of Thailand, as is the factor everywhere, is the Thai lifestyle, the norms, beliefs, ideas and superstitions. This lifestyle emanated from China, was influenced by India very largely and has had some impact from Burma, Laos and the neighbouring countries through trade, interchange of population and political shifts.

This lifestyle depends on the staple foods of rice and fish, the rivers, the maritime trade, the forests, elephants and minerals.

This has found expression in their jokes, proverbs, inhibitions, way of communicating with others, religiosity, social customs and manners. Their innate sense of hilarity has developed an appreciation of a joke at their own cost. This has been shown in their folk tales where the Chinese are shown as more crafty and prospering at the cost of the simplicity of the Thai farmer.

Their interpretation of the origin of the world, the meaning of dreams, their innate animistic slants, belief in the supernatural, mysticism, their belief in the earth as a mother, their various fertility rites associated with agricultural operations, their water festivals, their socio-religious ceremony of floating of the lighted paper-boats, etc., their unbroken veneration for Buddhism have naturally inspired or coloured many of their folk tales.

Superstitions have supplied the motifs for some of the folk tales. The river-ways in Thailand have encouraged large fleets of *sampans* (big boats). There is always some water on the hold of the boat above the last board. Collect the water from under the boards of the bottom of seven *sampans* and give some of it to an erring amorous husband and he will come back to his wife.

In Thailand dead bodies are not often disposed of immediately and are kept embalmed for future cremation at a convenient time. A sort of oil exudes from the dead body particularly due to the embalmment. Collect a small quantity of this oil and throw a bit of it on the girl who is not responding to your overtures of love. She will immediately return your love or go mad. There are folk stories in Thailand with this theme. Superstitions do play a part still even in educated families, just as they do elsewhere. For instance thirteen people will not still sit at a dinner table in an educated Christian family.

Witch and ghost stories and stories of the witch-doctors are common in Thailand. Thai ghosts love to pluck out the liver. In swampy regions the will-o'-the wisp phenomenon is taken as a spirit roaming about. Thorns and stones are strewn around the huts in such regions to make it difficult for the ghost to enter the house. It is believed that malevolent spirits can take the shape of a tiger or a snake and do harm.

Amulets and charms are in great demand. Medallions of Lord Buddha are commonly worn to keep danger away.

The witch-doctor stories are interesting. If a house is haunted even the educated Thai will arrange for a ceremony known as *Kruat Nam* or the water examination to propitiate the ancestors and sprinkle the water all round to exorcise the evil spirit.

Slavery was abolished by King Chulalongkorn or Rama V (1868 – 1910). There are folk stories about slavery like those in Arabia and other Mid-Eastern countries. Forced labour is now abolished but there are still folk stories about forced labour showing it as foolish and simple.

Astrology and alchemy have a strange hold on the Thais and there are humorous folk stories of cheats posing as astrologers or alchemists. A foolish son believed in alchemy. Before dying the father advised the son to collect some of the whitish substance found on the banana leaf and keep it in a pot and it would turn into gold. The son went on growing banana plants and his wife sold the bananas and made money. After some years when the required quantity of the whitish ash on the banana leaves was collected but it did not turn into gold, the man was perplexed.

The wife who had been taken into the secret by the father before he died pulled out the gold she had made by selling the bananas and disillusioned the foolish husband and gave away the secret that the father wanted his son to find out that alchemy is a fraud.

Miracles are still believed in and there are many folk tales describing miracles. In 1957 a five-star hotel, called Hotel Erawan, was being built by the government and repeated disasters followed. A steamer bringing in marble slabs from Italy sunk. The Thai government, on the advice of a Brahmin priest raised a small temple of Brahma (Phra Brahm) and after that all disasters ceased. The belief in miracles is very strong even now. Snakes crossing the road indicate good luck.

Nature's fury also finds its place in folk stories. Thunder and lightning form the background of the very popular story of Mekala and Ramasoon. The story is depicted in a dance which I saw. Mekala a beautiful girl born in the spume of the sea used to dance and fly about in the clouds with a crystal ball as her protector. Ramasoon was attracted by the beauty of Mekala. Whenever he tried to capture Mekala, she would turn the crystal ball towards Ramasoon and lightning followed by thunder claps would occur.

Even Buddhist Bhikkus do not escape the folklorists. Four robbers ran away from the prison and took the yellow robes of a Bhikku and went to a place far away. They cheated the villagers for a long time but were found out ultimately and beaten up.

The animal theme in the folk tales is common. Jackals are cunning and come in as the saviour in many folk tales. Monkeys are wily but kind to man — an influence of the Ramayana. Crows carry tales and pigeons and parrots carry messages. Elephants figure much more in the folk tales of Thailand than they do in India. This is due to the large elephant population in Thailand where white elephants are held sacred. Incidentally, Burma was once involved in a fight with Siam for the possession of white elephants.

Peculiarly enough, crabs, tortoises and fish so very common in Thailand do not figure largely in folk tales but snakes do. *Naga* (snake) stories are common in the folklore of Thailand. In the popular folk tale of Bandita the snake motif is prominent. This story has travelled to Malaysia.

The King and Queen do not figure normally in folk tales and

certainly not the King and Queen of Thailand. Veneration and love for them is incompatible with a folk tale about them. If at all, it must be the King in some other country or a petty king. Royalty is held in such veneration than in the past no one would dare touch or rescue a person belonging to royalty even if he or she were to drown.

The line of demarcation between folk tales and legends is thin. Some of the Thai folk tales and legends have been retold in compositions that have been recently hailed as literary master-pieces. One such is Phra Law — a romantic story of a king of a small country in the north of Thailand. Two beautiful princesses of an enemy country fell in love with this young and handsome king though married. The romantic king, however, was also drawn to the two princess because of their beauty and charm. Two maids of the princesses acted as the go-betweens and they also fell in love with the two romantic attendants of the romantic king. There could be no marriage as the princesses were of an enemy country.

A clandestine love affair developed. The grandmother of the two princesses came to know of the matter and sent some soldiers to kill the king and his two faithful attendants. These three along with the two princesses and the two maids were killed. This story though not exactly a folk tale has become very popular among young men and women. A changed version is current in the rural areas.

A story of Lord Buddha in his last but one birth on the earth is known as Mahachat and has been retold in verses by many poets. The pathos, humour and the descriptive scenes appeal to young educated boys and girls. This story is on the way to becoming a folk tale in the villages through the process of time.

Folk tales have also encouraged painting. In particular the stories of Mekala and Ramasoon, Khun Chang Khun Phaen, Phra Law, and the stories of Ramakien have been the themes of many paintings. King Rama II has retold the story of two men, Khun Chang Khun Phaen and Wan Thong, a woman. This version mentions many old customs and beliefs.

The royalty in Thailand has taken active interest in the pursuit of advancing culture. King Rama I's version of the Thai Ramayana is a literary gem and has been retold with beautiful illustrations. Some foreign and Thai folklorists and the Fine Arts Department — an active wing of the government — have taken up the work of preserving the folklore, mural painting, etc., of Thailand.

The imagination has given rise to some typical stories. There is the tale of the first banana tree which is more like a fairy tale. At Sri Maha Poh Province in Prachinburi lived Samoi, a beautiful damsel. One day she met a handsome young man near an enchanted cave. Both fell in love with each other. But after a few meetings the young man told her he was a wood-fairy but had taken human form and he was sad that he had to stop visiting her. The girl would not let him go willingly. The girl clutched his hand to stop him from going. Leaving his own hand in her hands the youth vanished. Samoi was horrified and quickly buried the hand at one corner of a field.

Next morning a peculiar plant appeared on the spot. Samoi nursed the plant by watering it. The plant grew with big smooth leaves. In a month it bore fruits in the shape of a long hand with many fingers. This was the first bunch of bananas according to the Thais. This old Siamese folk tale is unique, and as far as is known, has no counterpart in any neighbouring countries.

Animistic belief is at the base of the popular folk tale of the golden goby (a small fish with ventral fins joined to a disk sucker). The themes of the story are a deep faith in reincarnation and punishment for sins committed in one's previous life. The story also fits in with Buddhist doctrines and appeals to the Thai mind nurtured in Buddhism. The story narrates an unfortunate daughter's problems for no fault of her own with a scheming stepmother and their dire consequences. The harassed girl Uay was ultimately married to a king. Sethi the father of Uay and Kanithi the scheming stepmother were pardoned and allowed to come out of their hiding place and live at the court. The story explains that they suffered because of ill deeds in the past life. Uay had suffered also for the same reason. A wise man comes and explains to the king and Uay the meaning of the folk tale.

Some folk tales, like the seven-coloured emerald, Prince Tuang, Thong, etc., are often presented in the form of Likay, the most popular nationwide dramatic form. It may roughly be described as a rural opera. Villagers will gladly spend the whole night seeing a Likay and enjoy the popular folk tale probably for the hundredth time with the same sustained interest. Everything about Likay, the stage, the dress of the participants, the scenery (mostly non-existent), green room is unsophisticated, and make-shift. The audience has to presume a lot. Yet Likay keeps hundreds amused, if not enthralled. No temple-fairs in Thailand would be complete without Likay.

The plots in the Likays are a number of folk tales with the themes of love, villainy, the damsel in distress, her rescue by the valiant hero, etc. Some of the stories speak of the battle between Siam and Burma, the Mons and others. The female parts used to be performed by males but now some gallant girls have come forward. Gasoline canisters with a bamboo cover make an excellent stage.

Fantastic costumes and discussion between the lovers about the freezing weather (when all are perspiring because of the heat), but their love is warm, without any back-drop and showing others dressing, add to the hilarity. The dances are fairly basic. But there is no doubt that the Likays have kept many folk tales alive.

Folk tales are also kept up by the dance-dramas, a thing of joy in Thailand. Dance dramas are very diversified and the presentation is varied. Both smart hotels and rural areas have them but naturally the costumes, the lights and the presentations differ. The courts and the aristocracy patronised a few types like *Khon, Khon Lakorn, Nang,* etc. But now they have been extended to the peasantry. Western influence has had its impact.

The Ramakien, the Thai version of the Ramayana, supplies the stories for Khon where the actor-dancers are masked. Music is provided by a five-piece piphat band. the actor-dancers are trained from as young as the age of six. These dance-dramas are rather sophisticated and go on for about twenty hours and are staged on two successive days. The story has to go on till Rama is reborn.

Folk tales have not much chance in Khon. But in Khon Lakorn along with Ramakien and Jataka stories, folk tales are also the theme. The unmasked actors in their recital may make additions or subractions to amuse the audience.

In *Nang* or shadow-play where cowhide figures are held against a screen and shadows cast by light, folk tales have a place, unique in the history of Thai dramatic art.

Folk tales play a particular role in Thai culture and the Thai attitudes and appreciation of the norms of life are well expressed in them. It is good that there had been an attempt to preserve them by some scholars to whom I am indebted. The children enjoy them and the older folks are amused by them. A few such stories have been retold here.

It has been a privilege for me to have been so well received in Thailand. I cannot name all the many friends who had helped me in many ways. My doctor-son who is presently posted there and keenly interested in Thai culture took me hundreds of miles to absorb what I could. My friends over there fondly asked me to go there again. This is a small token of my love and regard for them and for Thailand.

P.C. Roy Chaudhury
New Delhi

# 1

## *Mekala and Ramasoon*

When clouds roll with thunder and lightning flashes
across the sky in Thailand, the child looks up and spreads
its tiny hands and shouts, 'There is Ramasoon's axe and
Mekala flees with the help of her crystal ball.'

This is one of the most popular Thai folk tales. The
traditional figures of Mekala with her crystal ball and
Ramasoon with his axe are known to every man and
woman in Thailand. Their picture is drawn on leather and
punched on rice-paper and sold in thousands.

Mekala (May-ka-la) was a beautiful nymph, born in
the frothing white foam of the sea. She was young, with
bewitching eyes, long black hair and had a gay manner.
She could fly and she often sported in the air, among the
clouds with her crystal ball in her hands. The crystal ball
protected her. At her will it spat out fearful blinding
flashes.

As Mekala had a rather quiet time in her palace she
would frequently slip out, fly through the layers of clouds
higher and higher up and play about. Often she would
be alone. She loved this sport. Also she would fly about
with her friends, all sparkling with jewels and in bright
and colourful clothes. Mekala would conceal the crystal
ball in her clothes.

The soft beauty and charm of Mekala attracted
Ramasoon, born in the storm-clouds and with rain as his
cloak. The greatest friend of Ramasoon was Rahoo the
god of darkness. Ramasoon always carried his axe as his

weapon. If Ramasoon wanted, he called Rahoo and there
was a thick cloak of darkness all round. Ramasoon had
the evil desire to grab Mekala and carry her away to his
den.

One day Mekala was sliding down and jumping up the
beautiful fluffy white clouds that lay high up in the sky.
Suddenly there was a thick layer of black and ominous
cloud rolling towards her. It was Ramasoon rushing to

grab the lovely nymph and Mekala understood his greedy eyes. The wicked Ramasoon kept himself well concealed under the cloak of the thick clouds but Mekala had seen him with her celestial eyes. She did not lose time. She brought out her crystal ball and willed the ball to send out blinding flashes. Ramasoon threw his deadly axe at Mekala to hurt her so that she could not fly away and there was a thundering crash and a deafening noise.

But Mekala's crystal ball did not fail her. After each flash she heard the axe crash and slip down the layers of dark cloud. Then came the heavy rain which Ramasoon desired and under its cloak Ramasoon escaped.

Mekala also hurried back to her beautiful palace. She untied her long dark hair and dried it. The crystal ball was put away safely.

Mekala, however, was not daunted. She continued her sport but always took the crystal ball with her. Ramasoon could never shake off his infatuation. He often tried to trap Mekala. He would throw the axe and Mekala would escape with the help of her crystal ball. This still goes on high up in the sky.

That is why we in the world hear the deafening crash of thunder when Ramasoon throws his axe and see the lightning when Mekala's crystal ball flashes blinding rays at his eyes; and the rain falls heavily to help the defeated Ramasoon escape.

# 2
## Manora

The King of the bird-people had his capital at Suwan Nakon (City of Gold) somewhere in the great forest of Himapun at the foot of the Himalaya mountains. The King had seven daughters and all the princesses were petite beauties dressed in glittering silken robes. Manora was the youngest and the most beautiful of all the sisters.

Every full moon the seven princesses loved to fly through the air to a lake near the hermitage of a monk. They took off their wings and tails and swam in the lake till the dawn. Just when the golden ball of the sun and its rays appeared they donned their wings and tails and flew home merrily.

This lake was near the kingdom of Pawnkala. A subject of the King of Pawnkala, named Bun was a great hunter. Once he had saved the life of the King of the Snakes and the King of the Snakes had promised to give Bun help if he ever needed it.

One night Bun was near the cave of the monk when he heard a soft swishing sound and concealed himself. He saw the seven bird-Princesses come down in a joyous mood. He saw them cast aside their wings and tails and get into the lake. Bun was smitten by their beauty.

Bun approached the hermit and asked him how he could catch one of the fairies and present her to his handsome Prince Sutone. The hermit said the only way to catch one was to apply the serpent noose of the King of the Snakes. Bun was elated. He approached the King of the Snakes and got the noose for him. The snake King also taught Bun how to use the noose effectively.

Bun waited for the next full moon, then he concealed himself behind a tree and held tight to the noose. When the Princesses came out of the waters and were getting ready to fly back Bun aimed at the most beautiful girl, Manora, and threw the noose. Manora was trapped. She tried hard to get out of the noose but failed. The other bird-princesses flew away sad at heart.

Bun picked up the feathers of Manora and took her to Prince Sutone. Sutone was handsome and young. He immediately fell in love with Manora and married her. But for quite a while Manora was very unhappy and thought of her home in the Himalayas and her celestial people there. But after some time she came to love Sutone deeply and forgot that she was *kinnaree*, a bird-Princess.

Pawnkala was attacked by a fierce army. Prince Sutone had to lead their army. He was sad to leave Manora but he had to do it. The King and Queen had to look after her.

Now Prince Sutone had an enemy in the royal court, the powerful Law Minister. For a long time the Law Minister had known that he could not sway Prince Sutone. His absence gave him the opportunity.

One night the King had a bad dream and asked the Minister what it meant. The Minister tried to look very wise and kept silent with his eyes shut for some time, as if he was trying to fathom the mystery of the bad dream. Meanwhile, he hatched a plan. He opened his eyes and told the King, 'Sire, I see death before you but you can surely escape if you make a great sacrifice of someone who is dear to you. It must be Manora. The spirits that are angry with you will only be satisfied if Manora is offered to them. There is no other way out.'

The King and Queen were horrified and wanted someone else to be sacrificed. But the oracle would not be moved and prophesied there was no other alternative. Manora heard all this. She told the King she was quite willing to be sacrificed to save the King's life but only wanted to give a farewell dance. And this was agreed to.

Manora put on her wings and feathers and started her superb dance. She looked sublime and her eyes shone. With every step of the exquisite dance her wings grew and became stronger. Suddenly she soared into the air and flew away to her father's palace in the lap of the Himalayas.

Prince Sutone achieved victory and came back after some time. He was told of what had happened to Manora. Prince Sutone put the wicked minister into a dungeon. Determined to trace Manora he repaired to the same hermit near the lake.

The hermit said: 'Prince, take this ring that Manora

left for you. I will also give you a monkey to guide you in the long and arduous journey covering seven years, seven months and seven days before you reach the destination. God bless you in your mission.' Sutone accepted the hermit's blessings and left the hermitage with the monkey. The journey was very arduous but the monkey guided him through hills and jungles.

After a very hazardous journey Sutone reached the bird-land. He was seated near a pool with his staff when some bird-maidens came and filled up their water jars. From the chit-chat of the bird maidens the Prince found out that the maidens were taking water for the ablution ceremony to wash away the last of the taint of human contact on Manora.

The monkey advised Sutone to put the ring in a jar. Sutone managed to put the ring in one of the water jars, without exciting the maiden's curiosity. But Manora had not forgotten Sutone and her heart was still with him. When the water was poured out over her, the ring fell into her lap. She recognised it and picked it up very joyfully.

Manora learnt from the bird-maidens that a handsome man, a stranger was sitting by the pool and had come near them. Manora went to her father and said that her husband had come after undergoing all kinds of hazards for seven years, seven months and seven days. She appealed to her father on his behalf.

The King had always been sad about what had happened to Manora. He sent for Prince Sutone. The Prince came and made a deep obeisance to the King and fell at his feet. The King was pleased with him but insisted that the Prince must identify Manora; he wanted to test Prince Sutone.

All the seven Princesses, dressed alike were seated in a circle. Sutone was bewildered at first. They all looked wonderfully alike and so beautiful. The Prince then noticed the small magic ring on the little finger of one of them. He felt a thrill and pointed out Manora.

Great were the rejoicings at the land of the bird-King. After a long farewell, Prince Sutone and Manora returned to Pawnkala. Sutone became the King of Pawnkala when the old King died. King Sutone and Queen Manora lived and reigned very happily. Every year they would visit the bird-land up in the Himalayas and spend a lovely time. The country of Pawnkala and the bird-kingdom formed great bonds of love and the bird-people loved to meet the men and women of the earth.

# 3

## *The seven-coloured emerald*

King Hongse Thong had two queens. The elder queen had borne him Princess Sroi Pradub and Prince Hongse Yout, the Crown Prince. The King's youngest son was Prince Hongse Noi born of the second queen.

King Hongse Thong had become very old. He decided to distribute the royal treasure among the sons because only a male could become the King. He gave nothing to his daughter.

The King had a beautiful, large seven-coloured emerald. He wanted to give it to the Crown Prince. The younger Prince was angry at this and complained to the father that instead of the seven-coloured emerald he did not get anything.

The King's younger brother sided with the second Prince. But the other nobles agreed with the King that the Crown Prince alone must get this family heirloom. There was a great split in the royal court. The story spread to the commoners.

However, a bold thief stole the seven-coloured emerald and neither of the Princes got it. The King was sore and the two Princes were bitter. But nothing could be done about it.

# 4

## The story of the two Chinese friends

One Chinese folk tale very popular in Thailand is the story of two poor Chinamen, Nguan Heng and Ha Yong. However much they toiled in their village in China they remained poor. Being much troubled by their poverty these two Chinamen of Swatew decided to come to Siam and turn over a new leaf. They had heard that Siam was a land of plenty.

In a junk they left their own inhospitable land and came to Bangkok, the capital. On the journey the rich emerald green rice fields welcomed them. They decided that they had taken the right decision and were very hopeful of a bright future. After a slow journey by river they reached Bangkok.

There they decided to separate and go in two different directions. They had made a solemn resolution that till they had amassed a good deal of money — not less than five hundred *bath*,* neither of them would eat pork or duck or chicken.

Nguan Heng took up a small job at one end of the town. He stuck to his resolution. He only took rice and salt and salted turnip. He would not even touch small fish that were plentiful and very cheap. He started working hard and saving his money from the very first day of his new life in Siam. He remained satisfied with rice, vegetables and noodles. He had a small business at

*Bath* is the common monetary unit in Thailand.

first and put his savings into the business. As he led a simple and austere life on principle he did not feel tempted by meat. Even when he started to prosper he would not indulge in pork or duck or fowl. He always remembered the resolution. But he was happy.

It was only when he had amassed much more than five hundred *baths* and he had built a house for himself and taken a wife that he started eating meat, fish and eggs. He became a prosperous merchant, well-known in his area.

Ha Yong stuck to the promise for only a fortnight. The dressed ducks displayed for sale became a great temptation to him. On the sixteenth day he though he would buy a duck, once and for all, and eat it. He solemnly told himself he must not buy one again as he was still trying to get on and his daily wages were not much.

He bought the duck and had a good feast, then he had a good sleep. Next morning the taste of the duck remained on his tongue and the whole day at work he thought of it. That evening he looked for another duck, one that had died of a disease and would be cheaper. But his search was futile. At last he bought a duck again and pacified himself with the thought that this would be his last one till he had put by five hundred *bath*. But he was just fooling himself.

Once a resolution is broken one goes on slipping more and more. The desire in Ha Yong to eat duck got the better of him and he went on buying ducks every day. Then, after some months, he thought that since he had been eating ducks for quite some time he might as well eat pork. So he started eating pork. And after a few more months he would eat duck, pork or fowl every day. He did not forget his resolution and was always trying to console himself with false excuses.

The expense made a big hole in his pocket. His earnings were small and all of that went on his food. Ha Yong remained almost as poor as he had been when he had come to Bangkok. He was a disappointed man. He wanted to meet his friend and see how he had fared.

He went to the town where Nhuan Heng lived. He asked some people and they directed him to a big house in an orchard. At first he would not believe it was Nguan Heng's place. He was greatly surprised when he met his friend at work and surrounded by people.

Nguan Heng saw the condition of his friend and particularly his clothes. In comparison he felt embarrassed as his friend's clothes were tattered and he had a hungry look. He did not put any further questions to Ha Yong. Nguan Heng spoke to his friend very kindly and offered him shelter and food.

Ha Yong was given a small hut in the garden to live in and his friend sent him rice and salted fish for his food. There were some tamarind trees in the garden. Nguan Heng told his friend he could pick some leaves off the smallest tamarind tree and boil them with his rice and salt as that would give a very good taste to the food. Within a few days, Ha Yong had picked out all the leaves of the smallest tree. He wanted permission to pick the leaves of some other tree.

His friend smiled and said, 'See what you have done to the tree; it is just what you have done to yourself. Instead of taking a few leaves from one branch and allowing the branch to grow fresh leaves, you have completely denuded the tree. It will now take a long time for the tamarind tree to be covered with leaves again. When you were to save and think of the future, you went on spending whatever you had earned and that is why you could not improve your lot. As for myself, I toiled hard, saved money and would not eat fish, meat or ducks till I had put by more than five hundred *bath* as we had decided. My friend, let this be a lesson to you.'

The lesson went home. Ha Yong mended his ways. He lived an austere life, worked hard and saved a lot of money. His friend guided him on how to do good business. Ha Yong was a prosperous man in a couple of years.

# 5

## *Asni and Kokila*

Two angels in heaven had a petty quarrel. Uma the wife of the God Siva punished them so that they had to be born as human beings in Suvannabhumi (Thailand).

So the two angels were born in a village in the land of Suvannabhumi. One became the daughter of a rich fisherman, not particularly beautiful but with a lovely singing voice. She was named Kokila the famous bird with a beautiful note. The other was born in a night when a strong tempest was blowing and the tide had flooded the pineapple orchard of the poor father. She was named Asni or the lightning. She was a sweet girl, graceful and gay.

Naturally Kokila was spoiled by her rich parents with presents and toys. Poor Asni had to work hard with her father tending the pineapple plantation. She never grumbled and was happy in her own way.

Once the rains did not come in the rainy season and everyone in the village that grew crops, vegetables and fruits was worried. The elders decided that the *Phra Pirun* (Varuna, the Goddess of Rain) had got to be propitiated by the customary ceremony of the cat. A black female cat was tied up and put in a basket and the basket was tied to a pole and carried over the shoulders of two boys. The cat was marched round the village accompanied by the beating of drums and songs. The elders seated themselves in the open space and started drinking while the younger ones performed the cat ceremony.

The cat was told in a song to ask for rain. As cats avoid water, the ceremony is performed to force the cat to induce the rains. The marchers went round a fire keeping their right side nearest to it. After three rounds they set the cat free. All the young girls danced in praise of Phra Pirun, asked forgiveness and begged for rains to pour.

Now in the audience was a handsome young man named Manop who came from the village but now lived in the town. His eyes fell on the beautiful damsel Asni and her graceful ways, her gentle and dignified steps in the dance, her laughing eyes and her supple body captivated the young man. Manop took the first opportunity to see Asni's parents and, after some chit-chat, asked about the welfare of Asni, his former play-mate.

Her old parents were very happy to see Manop after a long time, a fine young man of good physique and bearing and, from his clothes, they could make out that he was doing well in the town. They called out for Asni to come and pay respects to Manop, her elder brother (in Thailand it is usual for a girl to address an unrelated boy as brother as a sign of friendship). The two young people talked a little but Asni could see the message of love in Manop's eyes. Bashful as she was she excused herself as she had to help her mother and slipped away.

Kokila soon joined the other young boys and girls who came. They started gossiping, cracking jokes and eating, drinking and smoking the cigars wrapped up with lotus leaves.

Asni was asked to sing. She sang beautifully and everyone was enthralled. Kokila made out quickly that Manop was smitten with Asni and his eyes followed wherever Asni moved. She became extremely jealous.

A few days later Kokila was sitting on a rock when Manop threw the long rope to tie his boat without noticing her. The rope grazed Kokila's ankle and she called out pitifully to him. Manop was very apologetic and took her foot on his knee and carefully wrapped the ankle. The young man's heart was, of course, fluttering and Kokila was chuckling with glee at being so near Manop. They glanced at each other and Kokila made it clear to Manop that she loved him. Manop also thought Kokila had captivating ways and a very charming voice.

All this was the game being played by the goddess Uma who had banished the two angels from the heaven to be born as humans and taste the sweet and bitter fruit of love.

Manop was attracted to Kokila and started working for Kokila's father just to be near Kokila. Poor Asni's heart was full of pain but she had to gulp down her sorrow and carry on as usual helping her parents with the domestic chores and in tending the orchard.

One day Asni discovered a golden pineapple while working in the orchard. This was great news for the villagers. As is the custom if such a discovery is made Asni's parents presented it to the King. The King was pleased, gave presents to the parents and sent them away. The King found out that Asni was a young damsel of great beauty. He sent his messenger to the parents that the King wanted Asni at his palace.

The family was full of consternation at this order. But there was no way out. Everyone knew the King would sport with her youth and beauty for some time and then throw her away like an eaten fruit. But she had to go.

On the very first meeting Asni made it clear to the King that she loved someone else and that she could not love anyone else and that she should not be touched. The King tempted her, threatened her and then gave her some time to make up her mind. But at the second meeting Asni was still adamant and appealed to the King to spare her and send her back. She said if she committed a sin she would have to be reborn again and suffer. She did not want to do to the Queen what Kokila had done to her. The King was impressed with the girl's straight-forward talk and ordered that she should be sent back.

Asni came back to the village to find her parents dead, the orchard spoilt and the house looted. Bandits had come and killed her parents and ravaged the house. She left the house and met a villager who told her that, in spite of all Kokila's attempts, Manop did not ultimately return her love and he was still waiting for Asni. Kokila had tried to hang herself when she could not get Manop but people saved her and she was now dying of a grave illness.

Hearing this Asni ran as fast as she could to Manop's house. She took a buffalo-track, the night was dark but the stars were shining as the love in Asni's heart was glowing. Suddenly she stumbled over something, soft and warm, quivering and making a little noise. She found the dead body of a female-dog run over and killed by a buffalo-cart. There were seven tiny puppies lapping around the breast of the dead mother.

Asni put the puppies in her lap. A strange emptiness seized her as she found life and the world contained more sorrow. Her jealousy for Kokila vanished. She prayed and prayed that Kokila be her old self again and be united with Manop. She prayed that Uma should now take her back to heaven. She had had her cup of sorrow in the world and she felt she was now cleansed of her sins and she could go back.

The puppies were nestling against her now and she felt she had to do something to save them. She saw a light in a small house some distance away. She carried all the seven puppies to the house. She could smell the boiling rice. She could smell the salted fish, she thought of her parents, the loving house and the orchard. She thought of Manop, she thought of Kokila. She even thought of the King and wished him well for his gallantry in releasing her. She looked up to the heavens — she could see the outlines of the clouds, making the figure of Uma. Yes, Uma, the wife of Lord Siva was waiting to receive her back.

The inhabitants of the house heard a slight noise and came out with sticks and lamps thinking some strangers or dacoits had come. They saw a lovely girl sprawled out and seven puppies nestling against her body. Suddenly the peak of the Sabarb mountain was lit up — they heard the sound of tinkling bells and saw beautiful rays.

They saw a flash come out of the body of the girl and rise up. The flash changed into the form of Asni, this time in a celestial robe. Yes, she was dancing. They found the body had disappeared. Asni melted away behind the clouds while dancing to a sweet song. The great Uma received Asni's soul back as an angel. She had loved, she had suffered and she had atoned and was back again in heaven.

# 6

## *The story of Phikool Thong*

Phikook Thong was a princess. The name Phikool means a small, sweet-smelling yellow flower. Thong means gold. The girl was very handsome and was rightly named Phikool Thong.

One day Phikool Thong was on her way back from the river with her maids-in-waiting when she saw a vulture eating some carrion. Phikool told off the vulture about the foul smell and the maids agreed. They ran to get out of the stench of the place.

Now the vulture was none other than the King of the Vultures and he was much offended by the remarks of Phikool Thong. He wanted to take revenge by marrying her. By his magical power the Vulture-King made himself into a handsome youth and he took shelter in the house of a poor farmer.

After some time he persuaded the farmer to take him to the royal court. When he presented himself to King Sanuraj, Phikool Thong's father, the young man startled everyone by seeking the hand of the princess in marriage. The King checked his anger and thought he could easily solve this problem. He told the young man that if he could span the river by building a bridge across it in one night he would let his princess marry him. The young man agreed, but everyone thought he was mad.

Next morning the King was amazed to see a golden bridge shining over the river and people were joyfully walking over it. He was aghast. When the young man appeared, the King had to keep his promise and Phikool Thong was married to the young man. She accompanied her husband in tears and King Sanuraj was also very sad.

Through his magical powers again the King of the Vultures had made a palace some distance away. But Phikool Thong was haunted by a stench in the palace. Whenever her husband approached her the stench increased and she used to be sick. She could never allow her husband to touch her, without vomiting. She smelled the same stench a hundred times stronger that that she had smelled when she saw the carrion being devoured by the vulture.

The King of the Vultures wanted to teach the princess a lesson. He put her in a ship made by magic. The ship sailed and, when there was nothing ahead but the splashing waves of the sea, thick clouds came along. They were not really clouds but thousands and thousands of vultures and the husband of Phikool took the shape of a mighty vulture and started flapping above her. All the crew had become vultures and the ship was deserted but for Phikool. This was a trick to teach Phikool Thong a lesson and to make her submit to the Vulture King's evil wishes.

Phikool Thong prayed and prayed. Suddenly she heard a soft voice: 'My child, I am the goddess of the sea; do not fear. Hide yourself in the large hole in the spar of the main mast of the ship and I shall take care of you.'

Phikool saw the hole and got into it and the opening closed. She fell asleep and when she awoke she found a beautiful young lady in a *phasin* and *sabai*.* The goddess consoled her. She asked Phikool for a lock of her hair

*Traditional Siamese skirt consisting of two pieces of cloth, one upper and one for the lower part of the body. The *phasin* is wrapped round the waist and falls to the ankles, tied with a belt, often gold or silver. One end of the *sabai* is draped over to the left of the neck, leaving the right shoulder bare.

which was put in a golden locket and that was put in a golden sealed casket and thrown into the sea.

The locket reached a certain King Phichai when he was enjoying the evening sea-breeze in his ship. He had the golden casket brought and saw the locket with the lock of hair. He understood there was a lady in distress. King Phichai made for the ship where the Princess was in hiding.

On the way he was held up by Kakhao, an evil ogress who wanted the King to love her. King Phichai tricked her and continued his journey. He reached the deserted ship, tossed by the rough waves. As soon as he came aboard the ship the great hole opened up and Phikool Thong came out, a bashful young damsel, resplendent in beauty.

She told her story and begged King Phichai to take her away. King Phichai fell in love with the girl at first sight. Just then, the King of the Vultures appeared in the sky. He could not lay his hands on the captive princess now and so he must take revenge on her rescuer. But King Phichai killed the King of the Vultures with a poisoned dart from his great bow.

Phikool Thong was taken by King Phichai to his kingdom. They married and lived happily. She bore the king two sons, Luk and Yom.

But the ogress Kakhao whose overtures King Phichai had rejected was out to take revenge. One day Phikool Thong saw a lovely large lotus flower in the lake near the palace. She wanted to pick the flower, but the flower was none other than the ogress Kakhao. As soon as Phikool Thong plunged her hands in the water and touched the flower she was dragged into the water and changed into a gibbon.

The ogress took the shape of the queen (Phikool Thong) and went back to the palace. The King could not see that she was not Phikool Thong but her two boys felt she was a different woman. They had seen their mother going down to the river and told the father the story.

The boys would visit their mother, now a gibbon, every day. The King secretly followed the boys and saw the gibbon. The gibbon instructed the King that the ogress be killed and her blood be brought for her bath. Only then she could get back her original shape.

The King did as he was told. Phikool Thong became her old self. They all lived happily for ever in spite of other troubles brought on them by the sister of the ogress Kakhao.

# 7
## Prince Thep Thong
## (The golden-lanced prince)

Long, long ago there was a city named Kosampee ruled by King Thepmongkol. He was a great warrior and without a rival. The child of his first queen was Thep Thong. The King was getting old and wanted to leave the kingdom to Thep Thong.

Eleven of its provinces had been won over by the King, including Muang Tamin the province that had offered a great fight. But another town Muang Scrivachai was still unconquered. Before he died, King Thepmongkol wanted to win that town also. (Conquering other lands was a passion with many kings.)

The King and his son Thep Thong consulted the court astrologer as to whether the battle would be successful. The astrologer calculated and said, 'No, Sire, the circumstances are now ominous and a woman is involved. I suggest you do not try to win the town.'

But the King and his son did not listen to the astrologer but decided to march against the town.

Now Muang Srivachai had lost its King some time before. Princess Sroi Fah Thevi was the eldest princess and Prince Koot Chasing was the youngest but he had not been crowned yet as he was too young and inexperienced.

King Thepmongkol knew this and wanted to strike as he knew the army would not be properly led by the minor prince Koot Chasing.

When Muang Scrivachai was attacked the young prince

led the army but the army was defeated. The young prince was injured and died in the arms of the elder sister. Princess Sroi Fah resolved to take revenge. She disguised herself as a commoner and went about singing and dancing as if she was not at all concerned about the turns of the battle. Soon the town was won over and King Thepmongkol ordered his son to collect all the citizens and the precious objects together. While doing this the Prince met Sroi Fah and fell in love with her. He sent word to his father that he had met a beautiful girl and wanted to marry her.

The King was very angry at this and sent for the prisoner Sroi Fah. The clever girl was not daunted. The King was also smitten by her beauty, charm and songs. Neither the King nor his son knew who she was and thought she was a commoner.

Sroi Fah concealed her hatred well and went on singing to both the father and the son and behaved as if she loved both of them. She was allowed a room in the palace and treated lavishly.

One night when the King was asleep Sroi Fah slipped into his bed-chamber and slew him with her golden lance. After killing the King she went to the Prince's bed-chamber and killed him too. In this way she disposed of both the father and son and ran away. The deaths made the citizens bold; they revolted and she recaptured the town.

And so the astrologer's prediction was fulfilled.

# 8

## *The clever monkey*

A monkey got a thorn in his tail and could not get it out. The monkey went to a barber and said, 'Brother barber, please pull out the thorn and I will pay you well.' The barber wanted to get rid of the monkey as soon as possible. He used his razor and got out the thorn but in the process a bit of the tail was cut off.

The monkey was furious and demanded, 'Barber, barber, put back the bit of my tail or give me your razor.' The barber, of course, could not put back the portion of tail and parted with his razor. The monkey was glad that he had made a profit.

On the way home the monkey met an old woman who was cutting wood for fuel. The monkey told the woman, 'Granny, why not use my razor and cut the wood more easily?' The old woman was happy at the offer. But the razor broke soon. The monkey was in a rage; 'Granny, either give me back my razor as it was or give me all the firewood.'

Now the old woman could not possibly patch up the razor and had to part with all the firewood. The monkey marched off with his load of firewood.

Soon after the monkey met another very old woman making delicious fish-cakes by a fire. The monkey said, 'Granny, all your firewood is exhausted and some more cakes have to be made. Why not use some of my firewood?' The old woman thanked him and used the firewood he offered. When the last stick was burnt the cunning monkey was very angry and shouted, 'Now, now Granny, you have used up all my firewood, you have to give me all the cakes instead.' The old woman parted with the cakes.

The monkey gleefully made for his home with the cakes. Now the smell of the fish-cakes attracted some dogs that rushed at the monkey. The monkey jumped up a tree leaving all the cakes behind.

The dogs made a hearty meal of the fish-cakes.

# 9

## Sung Tong, the Shell Prince

Long, long ago there was a King and Queen who were very unhappy as they had no son.

The Queen had observed many religious ceremonies and had prayed and prayed for a son. Then there was great rejoicing when it was known that the Queen was expecting a child. But the Queen gave birth to a beautiful shell.

The King was persuaded by the other minor queens that the Queen was a witch and she would ruin the King if allowed to stay in the palace. The King drove away the Queen by putting her and the shell in a boat. After floating for a number of days the boat touched land on the edge of a great forest.

The distressed Queen got out of the boat with the shell. She met an elderly couple in the jungle and they invited her to stay with them and share their food and work in the vegetable garden, which she gladly accepted.

But the shell had actually concealed a beautiful baby boy. When the three adults went out, the child used to come out of the shell, play for some time and then get back into the shell. He would clean up the house. When he became big he would even cook their food.

The Queen, his mother suspected that there was something unusual about the shell. One day she concealed herself and saw the beautiful boy coming out of the shell. She came out of the hiding place and quickly destroyed the shell. She asked the boy to lead a normal life. She called the boy Prince Sung which means the shell.

But the story of Prince Sung reached the ears of the jealous minor queens and they set some wicked men to catch the Prince and kill him. The Serpent King who lived underground offered to help protect Prince Sung. Sung was put in the charge of an ogress in the form of a beautiful woman. She reared the child for fifteen years.

The ogress gave the prince a bath in a golden pool and his complexion became a bewitching gold. She had taught him a *mantra* by the reciting of which he could summon all the deer in the forest or all the fish in the water. She gave him a golden stick and a pair of golden slippers which helped fly him in the sky unseen. The ogress warned him of the danger he was in and gave him an ugly Ngoc costume which would hide his identity. He bade goodbye to the ogress and flew to the distant city of Samont.

The King of Samont had seven beautiful daughters. He wanted his daughters to choose their husbands and proclaimed that all the eligible young bachelors should come to Samont City so that his daughters could choose. The proclamation was sent to the kingdoms far and wide.

A day had been fixed. The story of the great beauty of the seven princesses had spread every where. Young princes from Cambodia, Laos, China, Burma, India, Malaysia and other countries assembled. All the young bachelors of Samont City had also been invited.

The day was bright and the King's court was beautifully decorated with flags and festoons of flowers. The princes from various countries and the other young aspirants were dressed in their best clothes and took their seats. The seven beautiful daughters of the King came out wearing dazzling costumes and jewellery. The first six of them chose their husbands but the seventh and youngest said she could not make her choice.

The King was angry and asked his minister if there was any one else left out. It was found that an ugly man in Ngoc costume had not come. The King ordered him to come and take his seat. Princess Rochana, the seventh daughter, was ordered to go round again and make her choice. She went round and could see the golden beauty of the boy under his Ngoc costume. She chose him. The King and the Queen were amazed at the choice and ordered her to go away and live at the outskirts of the city.

But the seventh princess Rochana knew she had not made a mistake. She lived happily in a hut with her husband who was still in that ugly costume. Rochana also did not tell him that she knew that beneath the ugly costume he was a youth of dazzling beauty.

The King did not like the idea of the Ngoc and wanted to get rid of him. He called all the new sons-in-law and ordered them to go out and hunt six deer by the evening of the next day. He wanted to test their hunting capabilities.

The Ngoc put on his golden shoes and flew to the part of the jungle full of deer. He muttered the words of the *mantra* taught to him, and changed the Ngoc form assuming his former golden beauty. All the deer came and rested near him.

Towards the evening the other sons-in-law came to that part of the forest. He changed back into the Ngoc form again quickly. The other princes begged him for six deer each. He said they could have one each but he would cut off a portion of their ears. They agreed.

The King was surprised when the Ngoc produced six deer while the other boys produced one deer each and that with its ear cut. The King flew into a temper and asked the sons-in-law to bring one hundred large fish of a particular variety next day. He wanted to test if the sons-in-law were good at fishing.

This was no problem to the Ngoc. He took off his disguise and sat by the river and muttered the words of the *mantra*. Soon all the fish came swimming to him. Towards the afternoon the six other princes and their servants arrived. This time to did not return to his Ngoc form. The other princes took him to the King of the fishes and requested him for some fish or else their father-in-law might put them to death. He agreed to give them two large fish each provided they allowed the tip of their noses to be cut. The princes had no other choice but to agree.

In the evening the six princes produced two fish each but the tips of their noses were gone. Their wives bewailed their lot as their husbands had lost a bit of the deers' ears the previous day. The Ngoc surprised every one by producing one hundred very large fish. The King and the Queen were bewildered. Rochana was happy.

But a harder ordeal was before the sons-in-law. The God Indra changed himself into a mighty soldier followed by his army and sent word to the King that he wanted to play a polo match and the city of Samont would be the prize. If the King did not accept the challenge the city would be burnt to ashes.

The King accepted the challenge. The whole court assembled at the pavilion. The King sent his six sons-in-law to play as he did not want to be humiliated by the Ngoc at the pavilion. The six princes were easily defeated. Indra told the King to produce his seventh son-in-law for the polo combat. The King and the Queen hurried to the hut of Rochana and the Ngoc and implored him to try and save the city. Rochana added her pleas to those of the King and the Queen.

Next day the whole city turned up to watch. Lord Indra in the garb of a huge soldier was there with his horse waiting to begin. There was no sign of the Ngoc. The King and the Queen were desperately wringing their hands. Suddenly a splendid horse flashed into the arena and seated on it was a prince with a golden complexion. He held the mallet like a very skilled player and challenged the disguised Indra.

The match began. The disguised Indra tried hard to defeat his rival but the latter was the better player. Indra's horse soared in the air and, to the astonishment of all, the seventh son-in-law also took his foaming steed into the air to meet the challenge. He had the golden slippers concealed in his flowing garments. The Lord Indra could not win but lost a goal. The game was over. The city was saved.

Rochana ran into the field and greeted her husband and patted the foaming horse. Lord Indra gave up his disguise. He came to the King and the Queen and said he was God Indra and wanted to tell them who the Ngoc

was. He was Prince Sung Tong and he would be the next King of Samont. Then the God disappeared.

Indra revealed the whereabouts of the lost Queen, Prince Sung's mother to his father. The old king rushed to the hut of the vegetable grower and found his queen there. The old couple were very handsomely rewarded with money, clothes and land. Prince Sung and his wife were united with his parents, and he became the next king of Samont as well as of his father's kingdom.

# 10
## Khun Chang and Khun Phaen

This is the story of the love of two men, Khun Chang and Khun Phaen for the same woman, Wan Thong. This story is more than a folktale now having been put in a great literary form. There have been many versions of different episodes in the story. King Rama II and Sunthorn Bhu, two of the great Thai poets, put many of the episodes in the style of everyday speech. The book has been translated into English and French.

Briefly the three characters lived in the same town and were playmates in their young days. The two lovers of the girl were of different types. Khun Chang was bald-headed, not good looking but very rich. He had married and went about as a country gentleman with a certain amount of bravado and a happy-go-lucky air. His wife died and Khun Chang tried to renew his old romance with Wan Thong.

Wan Thong had grown into a beautiful damsel. She did not like Khun Chang because of his lack of gallantry and his baldness. She had no interest in his wealth. She liked the other playmate of earlier days, although Khun Phaen was poor.

Khun Phaeng had left the town with his mother but had come back as a young man, full of gallantry and a sense of romance, a master of the magical arts of love and in warfare. Wan Thong's previous acquaintance ripened into deep love and they married. Khun Chang did not like it and was upset.

Some time later an insurrection broke out. Being a soldier of no mean merit, Khun Phaen was chosen by the King and sent to help suppress it. The husband and wife parted in tears.

During his absence the clever Khun Chang sent round a story that Khun Phaen had died in the campaign. He renewed his overtures of love. Just then Khun Phaen came back successful and with a title bestowed on him by the King. He had, however, found another wife and she came to the town with Khun Phaen.

This happened just a few days before the marriage of Khun Chang was due to take place with Wan Thong — although she had only agreed to the marriage much against her will because she thought Khun Phaen had died in the fight. Wan Thong and Khun Phaen's second wife had a bitter quarrel.

Next day Khun Chang forced Wan Thong to marry him although she protested that she was still the wife of Khun Phaen. Then Khun Phaen appeared on the scene and demanded Khun Chang to give back his wife. There were many epsodes in the story but ultimately Khun Phaen gave up his claim to Wan Thong.

The bare outline of this story is given because it is so well known all over Thailand. The three characters are vividly drawn in the story which is full of love, and humour and gives an idea of the old beliefs, manners and customs.

# 11

## The story of Prince Wichit and Princess Sno

Prince Wichit Chinda was the son of the King and Queen of Nakon Noparat, a beautiful city in Thailand.

On Prince Wichit's birth the court astrologer was consulted. He kept silent and sighed after making his calculations. The King insisted on knowing the reason. The astrologer said that in his previous life the Prince had killed a celestial *Naga* (snake). This evil action would pursue the Prince and at a certain stage of his life he would be dead for seven years, but he would be revived by a beautiful princess whom he would marry. The King and Queen thought this strange and reared the Prince with the greatest affection and care.

One day, however, the young Prince was sitting on a flat stone on the edge of the garden. A poisonous snake had left some venom on the stone, and Prince Wichit died immediately on touching the poison.

The King and the Queen were very distressed. The astrologer advised them to put the body of the Prince in a special pavilion in the garden. There he lay for seven years. The forest angels guarded the body. The Prince looked as charming and fresh as if he was alive and merely sleeping.

Destiny was at work all the time. In the neighbouring kingdom of Romanasai a beautiful girl was born to the King and the Queen. When the child was born the attendants saw a vision. The Princess was in a beautiful little house made from the tender fragrant plant known as Sno. Musicians were playing an enchanting tune and the newborn baby girl smiled. Then the miracle vanished. The parents named her Sno Noi Ruan Ngam which meant Little Sno of the Beautiful House. The baby girl grew into a lovely young girl of fifteen when the court astrologers were sent for to examine her destiny regarding marriage and the future. The court astrologers were amazed when they made their calculation. 'Oh King,' they said, 'this girl will bring ruin to the city and to you all unless she is banished at once. She is to marry a dead Prince whom she will be able to revive through some miracle. But she must be sent away immediately.'

The King and the Queen were distressed beyond words. But they could not possibly go against the astrologers. She was sent away to the jungle to work out her destiny.

The Princess was left in the thick jungle with a small bundle of clothes. She followed a bridle-path. God Indra could not remain uninvolved. He took the shape of an old hermit and met Princess Sno. Indra knew the destiny of the Princess Sno and Prince Wichit. He consoled the weeping child and told her to take courage.

'My child,' he said, 'take this medicine. In any illness rub a little of it on your forehead and you will be all right. If you come across a dead body you could even revive it by making a liquid out of the medicine, anointing and giving it a bath.' Princess Sno was surprised but kept the medicine. The old hermit vanished.

The Princess wandered in the forest and met an ugly woman called Kula. Kula was bitten by a snake and died. Princess Sno applied the medicine and revived her. Kula fell at her feet and wanted permission to follow her and nurse her. The Princess allowed this. But Kula was wicked and evil at heart. She wanted to know more about the medicine.

In their wanderings Princess Sno and Kula came to

Nakon Noparat. They came to hear of the Prince who had been lying dead in a pavilion for seven years. Princess Sno went into the garden and told the head gardener to take her to the pavilion.

The Princess told the men around to leave her alone. Kula, however, stayed on. The Princess took a bath and then in a religious state of mind made a liquid out of the medicine and anointed the Prince. At the end of the ceremony, she felt very hot as the fumes of the snake venom flowed out of him. She thought she would take another bath and feel cool. She left her royal dress and got into the pool. Kula was entrusted with the clothes.

On seeing signs of life in the dead body of the Prince a wicked idea crossed the mind of the evil Kula. She quickly changed and put on the royal robes. The Prince got up revived and heavenly music played. He saw the ugly Kula dressed like a princess and she assured him that it was she that had revived him.

On hearing the heavenly music Princess Sno ran to the pavilion and was amazed to see Kula in her dress. She demanded back the dress but Kula drove her away saying she was the maid servant.

Princess Sno had fallen in love with Prince Wichit and she did not want to leave him in the hands of Kula so she chose to remain as the slave.

The King and Queen were very happy at Prince Wichit's revival. They were very fond of Sno and suspected that she was being made a victim by Kula. But they could not turn away Kula. Prince Wichit was also suspicious and would not marry Kula in a hurry. Meanwhile, Sno had to live in a hut and look after the ducks and chickens and not talk with any one, under the orders of Kula.

Prince Wichit said that he would take a boat trip by the river before he married Kula. He sent a piece of cloth and some dye to Kula and asked her to make a pennant to tie at the prow of the boat. If she was a princess she would surely know how to make a pennant.

Kula did not know what to do. In her anger she tore the piece of cloth to bits and flung it out of the window. She threw away the basin of dye and the liquid colour flowed down the floor boards.

Sno collected the bits of cloth and the dripping dye. She sewed the pieces and used the dye and made a lovely little pennant. Kula snatched it away and beat her unconscious. She presented it to the Prince and said she had made it.

Prince Wichit suspected Kula but could do nothing. He wanted to sail but a strange thing happened. The anchor could not be lifted. The first mate told the Prince that the anchor could not be raised because the Prince had forgotten to ask the good people what presents they wanted. The Prince felt embarrassed as he had actually forgotten to do this.

The officials went round and asked the good people what they wanted. Kula wanted a big piece of red stone for a ring and others also put in their requests. Armed with the requests the Prince asked the first mate to set sail. But the anchor still would not move.

'Someone good has been left out,' he said. 'What about the girl who tends the ducks and chickens? She is a very good girl.' The government officials went to Sno and asked her what she wanted. 'Let the Prince ask for a beautiful little house of Sno wood,' said Sno, 'and that will be my present.'

A strange request Prince Wichit thought. The first mate was asked to lift anchor and the anchor was lifted easily. Wichit was now almost convinced that Kula was an impostor and Sno was the Princess who had revived him.

The ship visited the Kingdom of Romanasai. Prince Wichit made his purchases. He paid a visit to the King and Queen of Romanasai. But no one could buy a beautiful little house of Sno wood in the market. In despair, Prince Wichit asked the King of Romanasai if he could get a small house of Sno wood.

The King was overjoyed and felt certain that it was his daughter who had wanted it. He questioned Prince Wichit minutely and took the description of Sno who had wanted the little house of Sno wood. He knew Prince Wichit had been tricked.

However, he presented a little house of Sno wood to Wichit and sent two of his men to accompany Wichit in his ship and see the girl who had wanted it.

On reaching home Prince Wichit sent the little house of Sno wood to the slave girl along with the two men from Romanasai and followed them secretly. The two men recognised the slave girl as the Princess Sno at once and addressed her as such. Wichit was now convinced. He went and told his parents.

At midnight the little house of Sno turned into a big palace. Next morning Prince Wichit was surprised to see the palace. The doors were closed from inside. Prince Wichit said, 'If I am the destined husband of Princess Sno, let me enter and meet the Princess.' The doors were flung open and Prince Wichit went in and met Princess Sno. He heard the whole story from Princess Sno.

The King and Queen ordered the court to assemble. Kula was brought there and questioned. She knew her false story had been revealed and she confessed. She was ordered to be executed.

But Princess Sno had a soft heart and pleaded for Kula's life. Kula was sent away to a far off jungle and told she would be executed if she ever returned. Prince Wichit and Princess Sno were married with great pomp. They lived very happily for many many years.

# 12

## *Trees that have a meaning*

The lovely frangipani plant with its creamy white flowers is one of the charming ornaments of the garden. The tree is called *lanthom* in Thai and sounds very similar to the Thai word *rathom* which means sorrow. That is why the conventional Thais would not care to have frangipani in their compound. Many of the Thais associate the tree with death and believe the tree is the abode of the departed spirits, particularly those who were unhappy when alive.

Similar is the treatment of the soak tree. It is like not having an *ashok* tree in an Indian's compound as Sita had to stay in a forest of *ashok* trees when she was held captive by Ravana. Many conventional Indians still hesitate to name their daughters Sita, as Sita had more sorrows in her life than joys. The soak tree in a Thai compound is also viewed with some trepidation.

The rak tree is, on the other hand, much prized. The word *rak* means love in the Thai language. The flowers of the *rak* tree are woven into garlands and are worn round the necks of the bride and the bridegroom. But in the olden days the flowers were used as centrepieces for floral decorations at cremations. The older villagers in Thailand would not willingly have a *rak* tree in the compound for this reason.

The *ngiew* tree with its soft wood is very much prized for making coffins. That is why a *ngiew* tree is not looked on with favour in the compound. In the Buddhist stories of hell we also find the soft wood of the *ngiew* tree often mentioned. The tree has large thorns. The spirits of unfaithful wives have to climb this tree and be tortured in hell. Usually a large and ferocious tiger growls at the foot of the tree waiting for the spirit to slip and be devoured. No wonder if a *ngiew* tree is suddenly found growing in the compund the house-holder shudders.

*Phutarasaksa* or the lovely canna lily is not grown in the compound but as the fencing. Why? Because the lovely plants with their flowers keep away the evil spirits. The plants and flowers are largely used in religious ceremonies.

A very large tree is often taken as the abode of the spirits, good or bad. Offerings have to be made if such trees are cut. The large trees with thick branches and large leaves are the abode of male spirits. Large trees of medium size give shelter to female spirits.

The variety of banana tree called *gloo-ay-tanee* are the abodes of the infamous female spirits. The fruits have a lot of seeds and are not usually eaten. It is said that if you find a lovely young girl near this banana tree she is an evil female spirit. She will make love to you and you will feel tempted to visit her again. A few visits and your life-blood is sapped by the evil female spirit and you die a painful death.

If a young man starts becoming weak and emaciated he is carefully watched and prevented from going to such banana trees. The love-making is usually carried on in an unseen manner. Such evil female spirits are called Nang Tanee. They usually come out on lovely moonlit nights when young men get into a romantic mood.

Another evil plant which wreaks havoc if it happens to be planted near the house is Nang Yaem. Nang Yaem is an attractive shrub with branches of sweet smelling flowers. But in old age the spirit turns very annoying and would throw stones at the neighbouring houses when every one is asleep.

The *takian* tree is also to be avoided in the compound. The *takian* timber is used for making boats. Offerings have to be made before a *takian* tree is cut down. If the Nang Takian spirit is annoyed she will give out dreadful wailing sounds if proper homage is not paid to her. She is also a flirt and sings mournful songs to attract wandering men. The man goes to investigate and finds a lovely young damsel singing mournful dirges. He goes nearer and asks her what the trouble is. She will draw him into a fond embrace and squeeze out the life-blood.

# 13

## *The story of Prince Vessantara*

Almost every Thai has heard the story of the Mahachatt or Great Birth, the last of the Jatakas. This is recited at the close of lent in the *wats*. The story recited is in thirteen cantos and consists of 1,000 verses.

The main theme of the story is charity. Prince Vessantara was born to be generous. Even as a child he gave away the ornaments of his cradle. When he was a young man he was approached by some Brahmins from a drought-stricken area with the strange appeal to give away the sacred white elephant of the kingdom. Now the white elephant has the magic power to cause rain to fall and is a coveted treasure. The Prince did not hesitate to give away the sacred elephant.

But the citizens revolted at the gift. They persuaded the King to banish the Prince. Vessantara's wife, Madsi, his young son Jali and his daughter Kanha joined him. The exiled party was sent away in an ornamented chariot drawn by five horses. Vessantara gave away the horses to poor Brahmins that asked for them. The Gods changed themselves into deer and pulled the chariot till the Prince gave away the deer also.

Vessantara and his wife walked on foot, she holding the girl and he carrying the boy Jali. In their wanderings they passed by a town where the people asked them to stay on as the King and Queen. But the happy Prince refused.

The greatest test came later. An old Brahmin called Chujok had quarrelled with his young wife who refused to do domestic chores and particularly refused to fetch water from the well and insisted on the husband finding a servant. Chujok had no money. He thought of testing Vessantara's generosity by asking for his children. Chujok approached Vessantara, now in a hermitage leading a happy life, and asked him to give away the children to work as servants. Vessantara was shocked at first. Then he realised he had not so far given anything away which was a part of himself. He explained to his children his dilemma. The boy readily responded. Kanha was reluctant.

They were given away and to symbolize the act of the gift Vessantara poured water over the hands of the Brahmin while the children knelt before him.

The Brahmin took them away and treated them so cruelly that the children ran back to the hermitage. But Vessantara explained to them that a bargain made could not be broken. They had to go back to Chujok.

When Madsi the mother returned from the mountain and found the children gone she asked the husband. She fell into a death-like faint when she was told thay had been given away. The husband gently nursed her back to her senses and explained the sacrifice.

Sakka the God appeared as an old Brahmin and asked for Madsi. This was to test Vessantara. When Vessantara passed the test and agreed to give away his wife Sakka resumed his divine forms and returned Madsi. Thereby he bound her over to the care of Vessantara so that he could not give her away again.

Chujok lost the children who returned to their grand parents, the King and the Queen. The King heard the story and becomes very angry with his son Vessantara. But Jali explained the incidence of the great virtue of generosity and the King arranged to call back Vessantara and his wife from exile. He paid up the sum agreed for the ransom of the children and got the children released. Chujok spent the ransom money lavishly on wine, women and food and died of gluttony.

The King and the Queen went to the forest to bring Vessantara and Madsi back. They stayed at the hermitage for a month. A royal procession with decorated elephants and courtesans in royal attire, the soldiers in military dress went back to the capital with the King and Queen, Prince Vessantara and Madsi. There was a happy reunion of the royal family with the children at the court.*

---

*The main outlines of Mahachatt, so well-known all over Thailand are depicted in many sets of small paintings on cloth, paper or wood. The majority consists of thirteen illustrations, one for each of the thirteen cantos but there are also sets with a larger number. Wat Machimavas, Songkla, Wat Phra Luang near Praeh and the National Museum, Bangkok have some fine murals of this story.

As the paintings were done in late 18th century and early 19th century they show interesting local and extraneous elements in dress, facial features, general lifestyle, etc. The Tosachatt in Thai paintings is a great influence and that has made the stories almost like folk tales, known to everyone, young or old.

There are fine murals of the different stories in the Dhonburi area wats just across the river from Bangkok. Wat Suwannaram, Wat Dusit, Wat Daowaduengs, Wat Bangyikhan have some splendid murals of the Mahachatt stories. Wat Yai in Cholburi and Wat Machimavas in Songkla also have mural paintings.

# 14

## *The story of Mahajanaka**

The Boddhisattva was born as Prince Mahajanaka, son of a King of Mithila in India. The King was killed by his brother. His Queen was then pregnant. She escaped and a Brahmin of Kalacampa adopted her as his sister. Mahajanaka was born at the Brahmin's house and was reared there.

At the age of sixteen Mahajanaka came to know who he was. He took half his mother's jewels and boarded a ship and sailed for Suvannabhumi to make his fortune. The ship was wrecked. The Goddess of the Sea rescued him and carried him to a mango grove of the kingdom of the selfsame Mithila from where his mother had escaped.

But things had changed there. Polojanaka, the brother, who had killed the King, the father of Mahajanaka, had died. Sivali the Princess was at the helm of affairs and the throne would go to the person who married Sivali. But Sivali was very choosy and insisted on the suitor

*Some of the stories of the Jatakas have imperceptibly assumed the shape of folk tales in Thailand. This is mainly because wonderful mural paintings on the walls and the high ceilings of many old Thai *wats* all over the country have immortalised the stories. Groups of young children visit the *wats* and their senior companions or the teachers tell them the stories represented by the mural. Mothers and grandmothers repeat them to the young children before they fall to sleep.

The mural paintings are rooted in daily life and often show people working, playing, gossiping and even flirting and they appeal straight to the heart. Most of the *wats* were painted in the 18th and 19th centuries when literacy was rather rare. Some of the Thai mural paintings stand comparison in composition and execution with the acclaimed murals of Europe.

passing some tests. No one had appeared to try his fortune.

The ministers went out with the royal chariot to seek the King. The horses stopped near Mahajanaka who was deep in sleep. The ministers saw the auspicious marks of kingship of the soles of Mahajanaka's feet. They woke him and put him in the royal chariot. He passed the tests imposed by Sivali and they were married. They passed their days happily.

A son was born to Mahajanaka and Sivali and he was made the Viceroy. Mahajanaka had more time to devote to other work than the administration of the state. One day he noticed in the mango grove that the mango trees full of fruits were constantly plundered and the barren ones left alone.

This led him to thinking if worldly possessions brought in more sorrows. He was convinced if one desired less one lived a better life. He was sure that worldly possessions encouraged the desire to get more and more and led to more and more sorrows. Mahajanaka gave up the kingdom and became an ascetic though living in the palace. After four months he decided to renounce the world and became a hermit.

Sivali followed him and tried her utmost to dissuade him from his idea of becoming a homeless monk. There were army encounters but the King Mahajanaka ultimately vanished in the forest. The disconsolate Sivali returned to live the life of an ascetic in the royal gardens of Mithila.*

---

*At Wat Yai, Cholburi there is a beautiful mural painting of the shipwreck and rescue of the Prince Mahajanaka. The Prince is doggedly swimming amid fearsome sea monsters and fish. At Wat Kok, Dhonburi near Bangkok is the fine mural of the royal chariot stopping near the sleeping prince in a grove. The Prince is stretched out and the four ministers are sitting with folded hands.

# 15

## *The story of Mahanaradakassapa (another story of the Jatakas)*

Angati was the King of Videha. One beautiful moonlit spring night the King summoned three of his ministers and asked them what would be the best way of spending such pleasant hours.

The ministers gave various answers. Some said they should enjoy earthly pleasures to the utmost. Another suggested that the best way would be to listen to the words of a wiseman. The Minister Alata suggested they should consult the ascetic Guna.

But Guna was not wise. The King and his ministers met Guna in the deer park. The King asked how he might fulfil properly his duty towards parents, teachers, wife, children, the aged, monks, Brahmins, the army and peasants so that he could get into heaven.

Guna foolishly advised that there were no other worlds than this and so there were no consequences of sin and that it was no use being generous. Angati was overwhelmed by this wrong advice and embarked on a life of sheer pleasure.

The King had a daughter Ruja. She had a wiser head although very young and advised the King against the false instructions of Guna. She said that a man surely improves his lot by good deeds.

But the King would not give up his life of pleasure. Ruja prayed and prayed to the Gods to dissuade her father from his conduct. The great Boddhisattva took the guise of Narada and contacted the King. Through his counsel the King was eventually converted.*

*The Boddhisattva dressed in the hide of an antelope decorated with silver and carrying a golden bowl on a golden pole flies through the air to meet the King. In his bowl he has a lump of gold which he gives to the King to give away in alms and make merit. The King is seated on the throne and the young princess is praying. This is the backgrouind of the mural painting in gold and the black lacquer book chest at Wat Si Khom Kham, Payas.

At Wat Sutwannaram, Dhonburi there is the mural of the appearance of the Boddhisattva as the ascetic Narada.

# 16
## *The rose*

Thailand is the land of flowers and orchids. The Thai women with charming smiles on their faces love flowers. Presenting a bouquet of flowers is a common expression of love, affection and regard. Among the flowers, the rose is considered the most beautiful. The origin of the rose is from a woman and this folk tale is very common.

According to Thai tradition, a horde of gods and goddesses rule over the world. They are not super-creatures and have the elemental passions of love and anger although living in eternal happiness in different regions of the heaven way beyond the clouds in the sky. It is believed that by living a good life, and doing good to mankind, men and women can become gods and goddesses after death. If wicked and selfish in the world they will be reborn as animals.

When our story begins Sutep was a king among the gods in the kingdom of heaven. Sutep was unmarried. Young goddesses used to come and dance in his court. One day Sutep saw a beautiful young damsel of a goddess in his court and fell in love with her. The young goddess was Madhana. But Madhana could not be approached. Sutep's charioteer was his confidant. The charioteer tried hard but could not get an opportunity to pass on Sutep's message of love.

Sutep was desperate and consulted a great magician Mayavin. After making some calculations Mayavin said that in his previous life on earth as the King of Panjala,

Sutep had wanted to marry the daughter of the King of Surat who was now Madhana. The King of Surat had refused to marry his daughter to him and Sutep as the King of Panjala had attacked Surat and had captured the King of Surat.

The young daughter had appealed for mercy and said she would marry him if her father's life was spared. This the King of Panjala did but when he was about to marry her the young princess had committed suicide. The magician said because of the past enmity Sutep should give up the idea of marrying Madhana.

But Sutep was infatuated and implored the magician to do something and at least bring her to his court. The Mayavin performed some magic and Madhana was brought to Sutep in a trance. But whatever Sutep said to her she would simply repeat and she was like a stone statue so far as love was concerned.

The Mayavin told Sutep he could cast a magic spell on her and she would make love to Sutep but when the spell faded she would renounce him. Sutep would not agree to force the girl to love him in that clandestine manner. The Mayavin took off his spell.

Madhana was amazed when Sutep told her to wanted to marry her and stoutly refused. Sutep flew into a rage and banished her to be reborn in the world but promised if she wished to come back again to heaven to tell him she would marry him she would be brought back.

Madhana agreed but said, 'If that be so, let me be reborn as a beautiful flower. I shall be so happy.'

Sutep answered, 'You shall be reborn as a very beautiful flower that will enchant every man passing by you. On every night there is a full moon you will change into a lovely woman for a day and a night and then you will become a flower again.'

Madhana was sent away from heaven and was born

in the world as a rose with an exquisite colour and a captivating fragrance. A hermit Kalatatsin saw the rose in the forest and he had the rose tree transplanted to his hermitage.

Madhana as a beautiful rose was nursed by the old hermit and the rose tree thrived. Each night there was a full moon the rose would become a charming damsel and she would look to the comforts of the hermit. She looked upon the hermit as her father. Through his meditation the hermit knew her past.

The hermitage was in a forest in the kingdom of Hastina. On full-moon day King Chaiyasen of Hastina had come out hunting in the forest. Seeing the hermitage the King dismounted from his horse to pay his homage to the hermit. At the hermitage he saw the beautiful Madhana. They liked each other.

The King came again a few days later but did not see Madhana. The King questioned the hermit and came to know of Madhana's ill fate.

The King came on the next full moon and the hermit gave Madhana as his wife. The King took away the rose tree carefully and transplanted it near his bed chamber. Every full moon the rose flower would become Madhana and the King would spend a very happy twenty-four hours.

But the King had a wife Queen Chantee. She came to know of the rose that would change into a woman every full-moon. She was very jealous and sent word to her father the King of Magadha. The King of Magadha wanted to teach a lesson to Chaiyasen and attacked his kingdom with a large army. King Chaiyasen made arrangements for the protection of the rose tree and took out his army to fight the King of Magadha.

While Chaiyasen was away Queen Chantee played a cruel trick. She got hold of a wicked old man Vitun and asked him to go through some sham rituals near the rose tree and to tell King Chaiyasen that he was trying to make a love potion for Madhana and she loved a young captain in the army, Supang so that Supang, who was unresponsive, would reciprocate Madhana's love.

Setting Vitun to do his mumbo-jumbo Queen Chantee sent for the King on the pretext that Madhana was ill on a full-moon day. The King hurried back and asked Vitun what was he doing. The wicked Vitun repeated the story the Queen had taught him.

The King flew into a rage and, without even hearing Madhana, banished Supang and Madhana to the forests to be executed.

Some time later an old man was brought to the King suspected of being a spy. This old man was none other than Vitun. Vitun made a confession and said Madhana was as pure as the rose and it was Queen Chantee who wanted to get rid of Madhana. The King was full of remorse and wanted to inflict a severe injury on him with his sword.

At this moment Lord Teevanta revealed himself to the King and said Madhana had not been executed at all but only left in the jungle. He also said that the faithful Supang had come back and in disguise had fought for the King and had met with a glorious death.

The King routed the King of Magadha in the fight. He ordered a search for Madhana. He found out that Madhana in her distress had prayed to Sutep the King of Gods to come to her help. Sutep was very glad and wanted to take Madhana back to the heaven as his wife. But the faithful Madhana said she must remain in the world and wanted Sutep to help her to regain the King's love.

At this Sutep was very angry. He cursed Madhana to remain for ever in the world as a beautiful rose and said she would never become a woman even on a full-moon day. Because of this curse Madhana was changed permanently into a rose.

The King brought back the rose tree and transplanted it again near his bed chamber. But Madhana remained a perpetual rose superb in beauty and in fragrance.

Since then the rose has represented all that is best in a woman — softness, grace, beauty and fragrance. The rose represents the true tender love and fidelity of a woman. The rose has, since then, been the delight of men and the glory of women. The Thai girl in her teens is compared to a budding rose and the woman to a rose in bloom. An exchange of a rose between a boy and a girl is an expression of their love and regard.

# 17

## *The story behind Nakhon Pathom Pagoda*

Many of the ancient *wats*, monasteries and pagodas in Thailand have stories and legends associated with them. This is so in India too. The magnificent Konarak Temple in Orissa dedicated to the Sun God or the great Somnath Temple in Gujarat have stories as to their origin. On the road to Huahin-on-Sea, about sixty kilometres away from Bangkok is the largest golden Pagoda in Thailand. The road (Highway 4) passes through lush fields on either side, lined by sugar palms with their large fan-shaped leaves. Five kilometres before Nakhon Pathom one can see the high *chedi* with its golden top. This is considered the oldest Buddhist monument and the site is at least two thousand years old; the old town of Nakhon Pathom was probably founded more than a century before the Christian era.

It was the capital of a Mon kingdom with the name of Nakhon Chaisi. The old town had been decaying till King Mongkut, Rama IV wanted to restore the magnificent old edifice. Finding it in poor shape the monarch decided to cover it with an enormous cupola in the form of an overturned bowl covered with glazed tiles and topped with a ringed cone. The work began in 1853 and continued right through the reign of King Chualongkorn, Rama V until it was completed.

Nakhon Pathom is now an object of pilgrimage and of great tourist interest. It is an expanding town and has

a great future. This is the story of the origin of the first building.

The King of the land where Nakhon Pathom is located was Phya Kong in the ancient days. A son was born to the King and the Queen to their great happiness. As usual a number of learned astrologers were brought in to forecast the future of the royal Prince. The astrologers were aghast when they studied the position of the stars at the time of the birth of the Prince. They kept quiet and would not tell the King anything.

The King insisted and after assuring the astrologers that they would not be punished the astrologers relented. They told the King that their separate calculations showed the Prince was the killer of the King and he should immediately be banished to some far-off region or he should be put to death. The parents were astonished. But they could not bring themselves to kill the infant.

They put the child on a raft and the raft floated down the swift river. They thought the child would die out of sheer neglect and starvation if not devoured by fish or other aquatic animals.

Fate had ordained otherwise. The raft got stuck in front

of a small hut by the river side. The master of the house was Choma whose wife was Homa. They had no child and they happily adopted the infant. The infant grew under the tender care of father Choma and mother Homa.

The child was lovely to look at. The couple decided to make a present of the child to the King of Rataburi. The King adopted the child and brought him up as a Prince. The boy learnt the art of hunting and fighting. Rataburi was under Kanburi the King of which area was Phay Kong, the real father of the Prince.

Rataburi used to give three artificial trees of gold and three of silver to acknowledge the vassalage. The boy who was named Phya Pan had grown into a skilful warrior and advised his adopted father to stop giving this yearly tribute.

Unwillingly the adopted father agreed after warning Phya Pan this would mean rebellion and an open invitation for a fight. Phya Pan was itching for a fight little knowing his relationship with Phya Kong the King of Kanburi.

Phya Kong took his army and there was a strong resistance by Phya Pan. Phya Pan rode an elephant and challenged Phya Kong to a single-handed encounter which he accepted. In the bitter fight Phya Kong's elephant beat a retreat and Phya Kong was cut dead by Phya Pan.

Phya Pan occupied Kanburi. According to the custom of the country, the victor could force the chief queen of the vanquished king into marriage. Phya Pan declared his intention to marry the chief queen who was in fact his mother. He entered the palace of Phya Kong but he had strange forebodings. Something whispered to him that he was going to force his mother to be his wife. With this strange and oppressive foreboding he approached the widowed queen. Milk streamed out of the Queen's breasts and flowed into his mouth. He then understood the foreboding.

The Queen recognised him as her son from a scar on his face. The baby had been put in a golden tray for a bath and the sharp corner of the tray had wounded the face and there was a bleeding scar due to the negligence of the royal maids. Phya Pan fell at his mother's feet and begged her pardon.

Great remorse for killing his own father drove Phya Pan mad. He blamed Mother Homa for not telling him he was found on a raft. He rushed to the village where Mother Homa stayed. Mother Homa was very happy to see Phya Pan but the latter killed her with one stroke of his sword.

But later in his calmer thoughts Phya Pan was crazed over the two dastardly crimes he had committed. He had killed his father. He had killed the poor woman who had saved him from sure death and brought him up.

He consulted some Buddhist monks as to what he should do to atone: should he commit suicide? The wise and saintly monks told him, 'No, son, committing suicide will be the third and final crime for you. Thereby you gain nothing. Build a pagoda, the tallest in the land, out of humility and dedicate it to Lord Buddha. That alone can give you consolation and help you to atone.'

Phya Pan accepted the advice. He spent a fortune building the tallest pagoda in the land and in it was embedded the sacred tooth of Buddha.

All this happened during the time of Emperor Asoka who sent out several relics of Buddha to different places to propagate the *dharmma* of Buddha. Phya Pan raised another pagoda called Phra Pratone in memory of Mother Homa near Phra Pathom Chedi (the first pagoda).

# 18

## *The story of Totsakan (Ravana)*

Ramakian (Ramayana) is the story of the reincarnation of the God Narai (Narayana) on earth. Narai was sent from Heaven by Shiva to fight the power of evil under the leadership of Totsakan, the ten-headed giant (Ravana). Ravana was the reincarnation of Nonduk and had inherited the throne of Lanka.

Before Nonduk was born as Ravana he was a giant serving Shiva the supreme God in heaven. It was his duty to sit at the foot of Krailat Hill (Kailash Hill). Lord Shiva resided at the top of the Krailat Hill. When the gods and goddesses used to climb up the steps of the Krailat Hill to pay homage to Shiva, it was Nonduk's duty to wash their feet.

But the gods and goddesses loved to tease Nonduk. They would push and pinch him and used to pull out hairs from his head. Nonduk became bald, he got fed up with their teasing.

One day Nonduk went up to Shiva and, after paying him homage, prayed for a gift. Shiva gave him a gift and said his forefinger would become as hard as diamond, with the power of death when pointed at any one.

When next some gods and goddesses came and teased him, Nonduk became angry and pointed his forefinger at them. Some of the gods and goddesses fell down dead and a few managed to fly away. Shiva was approached. Shiva asked Narayana to go down and kill Nonduk.

Narayana thought of a trick. He took the shape of a

beautiful dancing goddess. Nonduk fell in love and danced with her. Narayana was careful that Nonduk should not point his forefinger at him but managed it cleverly so that Nonduk's forefinger was pointed straight at his own heart. As a result Nonduk went into his death-throes.

He saw Narayana changing into his own self. Nonduk jeered at him because he had had to take to a ruse and dared not fight straight. Narayana said he was not afraid and he would be reborn as an ordinary man with two hands and fight him when Nonduk would be reborn with ten heads and twenty arms. Then Nonduk died.

That is how Nonduk was reborn as Ravana, son of Lastian, the King of Lanka. He had a fierce look and had ten heads and twenty arms. He did *tapashya* and had acquired some supernatural power too. But it was ordained he should personify evil and that is what he did. Ravana was also known as Tutkhorn.

Ravana had two brothers, Kumpakarn and Bhibek and one sister Samanakkha. Kumpakarn and Bhibek loved justice. Bhibek had the gift of foretelling events; he could see the course events would take. Samanakkha was a wicked girl and always on the look out for handsome men.

When Totsakan (Ravana) grew up, he studied the magic arts of war from Kobut, a great hermit. One day Ravana strayed into an orchard and he plucked the fruits and damaged the garden. The orchard belonged to the god Orajun. On coming back Orajun found Ravana and as Ravana would not apologise they fought. Ravana was caught and tied up and put to shame. His teacher Kobut heard of it and got Ravana released after he had made his apology. Ravana swore to take revenge.

A giant of the underworld Virunhok once came to pay respect to Shiva. He used to come seven times a year to pay this homage. He would stop at every step of the Krailat mountains and make an obeisance by putting his head on the step. A lizard nearby thought this was very funny and laughed jeeringly. Virunhok got very angry and hurled his fiery disc at the lizard. The disc struck the mountain on one side with great force and the mountain tilted.

Shiva was aroused from his sleep by this sudden movement of the mountain. He sent for Ravana and asked him to pull up the mountain and promised him rewards. Ravana transformed himself into a huge body as big as the mountain itself and pushed the Krailat Hills with his twenty powerful arms and his feet propped against the earth. The mountain was put back to its original position.

Lord Shiva was very pleased and asked Ravana to name his gift. Insolently Ravana wanted Uma, Lord Shiva's spouse. Shiva could not refuse and requested Uma to accompany Ravana. Both Lord Shiva and the divine Uma smiled at the impudence of Ravana.

But Uma the divine mother of all gods could not be touched by any one excepting Shiva. Glowing hot rays would radiate from her celestial body which prevented Ravana coming anywhere near her. Ravana craved Shiva's pardon and exchanged her for Nang Monto a beautiful girl. Ravana was smitten by the beauty of Monto.

While Ravana was carrying Monto through the air he had to fly over the top of Khidkhin City, where Palee was the ruler. Palee felt offended that any one should go over his head. Palee fought with Ravana, defeated him and took away Monto. The defeated Ravana went back to Lanka humiliated and depressed.

Kumpakarn and Bhibek found Ravana very distressed and wanted to help him. They approached Ravana's teacher Kobut and on Kobut's advice approached Ongkot, Palee's teacher.

Ongkot intervened and said that Shiva would be very angry if he came to know of Palee's misdeed. So Monto was given up by Palee. Monto was then expecting a child and the unborn child was taken out from Monto's belly and put into that of a goat. Nang Monto lived on in Lanka as Ravana's wife.

When the child of Monto came out of the goat's belly he was named Ongkot after his teacher. Ravana wanted to take revenge on Palee. When the child Ongkot was being given a ceremonial bath Ravana took the shape of a crab and wanted to bite the child and kill him. Palee knew of the plot and caught hold of the crab. Ravana had to take his own shape when Palee tried to kill the crab. But Palee caught hold of him and assaulted him. After some time Ravana was set free, but he felt very humiliated.

Ravana then went to his teacher Kobut and asked him for more fighting powers. The hermit took Ravana's soul out of his body, put it in a glass case under lock and key in the hermitage and said henceforth no one could kill him unless the soul in the glass case was taken out and crushed.

From then on Ravana's head was turned and he became very insolent. He became very amorous too. He became a nuisance and a menace. He took the disguise of Indra, King of the Gods and stole the love of many goddesses. He took the shape of animals and a fish and had offspring in the animal and the fish world. In his own palace at Lanka he had many wives besides Monto the chief queen. He had one thousand children.

Monto's son was named Ronapak and this name was later changed to Intarchit (Indrajit). Ronapak was sent to the same Kobut, Ravana's teacher for education.

Kobut taught him much more than he had taught Ravana.
Kobut made the great gods Shiva, Indra and Narayana
give formidable weapons and a blessing to Ronapak that
if he was killed and his head touched the ground, the
whole world would burst into flames.

Ravana had forgotten himself in his pride. He sent his
son Ronapak to attack Indra in heaven. Even Indra could
not defeat Ronapak and had to fly back and conceal
himself in his palace. After this the boy was named
Intarchit — the conqueror of Indra.

King Tosarat of Ayudhya had as his queens Kaosuriya,
Kaiyakesi and Samutra. Once in a fierce fight between
a wicked and powerful giant Patutatan and Tosarat,
Kaiyakesi had saved the life of the king and helped him
deal a fatal blow to the giant. The king promised
Kaiyakesi that if she ever wanted anything she would not
be refused.

King Tosarat had no children and this was a cause of
great sorrow. The gods were also unhappy that the giants
in the world were becoming too powerful for any men.
The gods held an assembly and decided to request Shiva
that the time has now arrived for the God Narayana to
be born on earth to save men, women and the ascetics
in the hermitages. The Lord Shiva agreed.

Narayana was born to Queen Kaosuriya and was
named Rama. Three more sons were subsequently born
and called Lakshman, Barata and Satru. The last two
were born to Queen Kaiyakesi.

Lakshmi, Narayana's consort was born in Lanka to
Monto, Ravana's queen. When she was born she shrieked
ominous cries. Bhibek, the astrologer prophesied that the
girl would cause destruction to Lanka and the death of
the race of the giants. It was decided that she should not
be reared. She was put in a glass bowl and floated down
the stream.

The hermit Janaka found the infant girl floating down the river. He picked up the infant and brought her up. She was named Sita. The hermit Janaka was really the King of Mithila. As he had no children he had become disgusted with life and had become a hermit. Now that he had a beautiful girl as his daughter he went back to his kingdom and resumed his role as the king of Mithila. Day by day Sita grew into a very handsome girl.

King Janaka wanted Sita to be married. He had a famous and very heavy bow and it was impossible for any ordinary man to lift the bow and string an arrow to it. The bow was a gift from Shiva. Janaka had given out that if any one could lift the bow and shoot an arrow from it he would give away Sita in marriage to him.

A date was fixed and princes from far and near came to Mithila to try the bow. Rama and Lakshman, sons of King Tosarath came there too. No one except Rama could lift the bow and throw an arrow.

It was decided that Sita should marry Rama. The boy and girl looked at each other and their hearts melted with love. The marriage took place with great pomp.

Soon after his marriage Rama came in conflict with the great giant Ramasoon who causes thunder and rain. Tosaroth was going back with Rama and Sita accompanied by an army. While crossing a large forest they had to go through an area where Ramasoon was moving about. On seeing Tosarath's advance guards he took offence and attacked them. Ramasoon was told by Rama who he was. Ramasoon shouted how dared he have a part of his name and wanted to punish him by taking away Sita. At this insolence Rama challenged Ramasoon and gave him a good beating. Ramasoon acknowledged defeat, sought Rama's pardon and got his release.

## Rama's Banishment

King Tosarath had already grown old and wanted Rama to sit on the throne and so that he could go to the forests to lead a hermit's life of peace and prayer. But the queen Kaiyakesi intervened. She wanted her son Barata to come to the throne for fourteen years first and Rama could come after that period. Kaiyakesi reminded the King of his promise to grant her any wish.

All the entreaties of the King Tosarath and others that Rama being the eldest had the right to be the King fell on deaf ears of Kaiyakesi. Rama said he must see to his father's promise being honoured and that he would go away. Barata was devoted to Rama and did not want him to go. But he was helpless.

Sita followed Rama in his banishment; Lakshman said he must go with Rama. The three left the city of Ayudhaya and went to the forests beyond the Satakut Mountains. At one spot they found golden rose-apples and the three plucked the apples and ate them.

Pirap a wicked giant lived in the forest. He came back and found a number of apples gone. He became furious. The giant Pirap saw Sita who was sleeping and quietly stole her away. Rama and Lakshman woke up and fought with the giant and killed him. They recovered Sita and left the forest and moved on to Godavari River. They found a nice hut which had been built by the God Indra to welcome them. They stayed at this hut.

But Rama's encounters with the giants were not to stop. Ravana's sister Samanakkha who had lost her husband saw Rama when he was coming back from his bath. The giantess wanted to make love to Rama. Rama told her to go away. The giantess persisted and followed Rama. When she saw Sita she became very jealous and attacked her. Rama and Lakshman came to Sita's rescue and punished the giantess Samanakkha by slicing off her nose and ears.

Samanakkha went to her brother Phya Khorn who ruled at Romakel City. Phya Khorn was told by the giantess that Rama had been courting her but when she did not yield to Rama's desires she was treated like this. Phya Khorn believed this false story. He raised an army and attacked Rama. In the fight Phya Khorn and his brother Phya Tut were killed.

Some of the army fled to Phya Trisian, another great giant and a friend of Phya Tut and told them what had happened. Phya Trisian came with an army and attacked Rama. He made himself and his army invisible behind thick dark clouds. But Rama shot an arrow through the sky and killed Trisian. His army was routed.

The giant world was much perturbed. Samanakkha went to Lanka and gave the news of the death of the great giant rulers to Ravana. Ravana was incensed. She also told Ravana that Rama's wife Sita was very beautiful, more beautiful then Queen Monto herself. She tried in every way to inflame Ravana's anger and curiosity. Ravana wanted to win over Sita. Queen Monto tried to stop Ravana's wicked ideas about Sita. But when Samanakkha told Ravana that Sita was much more beautiful than Uma a consort of Shiva and Suraswadee — Queen of Love and Lakshami the wife of Narayana, Ravana decided to steal Sita.

**How Ravana stole away Sita**

Ravana wanted Mareet, son of Kakanasun, who was killed by Rama, to change into a beautiful golden hind and graze near the hut of Rama and Sita. He was sure that Sita would like to have the golden hind and Rama would try to take the hind captive. He instructed Mareet to run away further and take Rama far away from the hermitage. At some distance he should simulate Rama's voice and cry out as if Rama was in distress and then Lakshman was also bound to leave the hut to help Rama and that would be an opportune time for Ravana to appear and abduct Sita by force.

This plan worked out very well. Both Rama and Lakshman left Sita alone in the hermitage and went far away following the golden hind. Just then Ravana appeared as an old hermit and begged alms from Sita. When Sita came out to give alms the wily Ravana disguised as a hermit engaged Sita in conversation. He told Sita that she should not waste herself in the forest leading a miserable existence — she could easily live with Ravana a rich and powerful king more worthy of her. Sita spurned the suggestion and asked him to go away.

At this Ravana assumed his true shape and seized Sita by force and carried her off through the air and started for Lanka. Sadayu, a huge bird, saw Ravana carrying away Sita and attacked him. But Ravana cut off Sadayu's wings and the bird fell down on the earth. Sita threw her ring to Sadayu so that she could give it to Rama. Ravana took Sita to Lanka and put her in a garden and put his one thousand sons to guard the palace. Sita firmly rejected Ravana's request to be his queen.

On their return Rama and Lakshman found no trace of Sita. They started a search and met Sadayu who told them what had happened. The bird gave Sita's ring to Rama and then passed away. Rama and Lakshman cremated the bird. They came to Katliwan forest and rested there.

Hanuman the nephew of Palee and Palee's brother Sugriva had been turned out by Palee and lived in the

forest of Katliwan. Hanuman met Rama, paid homage
and offered his services. Hanuman was leading a life of
renunciation but he knew that Rama would come there
one day.

Rama saw the invisible diamond of hair of Hanuman
which Lakshman could not make out. (Hanuman had
been told by his mother that one who could make out
his invisible diamond of hair would be no one else but
Rama the incarnation of Narayana.)

Sugriva also joined Rama and raised an army from
Khidkhin. There was a fight between Palee and Sugriva
and Rama helped Sugriva by killing Palee with an arrow.
The King Chompoo also agreed to help Rama. Thus
Rama's army grew formidable in number.

Rama asked Hanuman to go ahead to Lanka with
Chompoo and Ongkot and find Sita and tell her that
Rama was coming with an army to fight Ravana and free
her. Rama made over Sita's ring which Sadayu had given
back to Rama to show Sita in case she did not believe
Hanuman.

Hanuman and his two friends made for Lanka. On the
way they met many troubles but came successfully
through the ordeals. They met a hermit Chadil who
pointed the way to Hamatiwan Mountain on the sea-shore
— just opposite the island where Lanka City was situated.
In a cave at this mountain lived a huge bird Sampatee
elder brother of Sadayu.

When very young Sadayu mistook the rising sun for
a golden apple and tried to reach it — the Sun God got
very angry about this and tried to burn up Sadayu.
Sampatee intervened but all his feathers were burnt up.
The Sun God had told him he would get the feathers back
when Rama's men met him.

Hearing that Rama's emissary Hanuman had come to
the mountains, Sampatee met him and got back all his

feathers. Sampatee carried Hanuman on his back and flew over Nikala Hills in the middle of the island and pointed out the City of Lanka nestling on the hill.

Hanuman said he would go to Lanka alone. He met the guardian spirit of the City of Lanka, a giant with four faces. Hanuman was involved in a fight with him and managed to kill him. At night Hanuman took the disguise of a citizen of Lanka. Hanuman hypnotized the whole city and when all the men, women and the children, the animals and birds were snoring in a hypnotic trance Hanuman got into the palace. He saw Ravana, his queen, the maids sleeping and went from room to room but failed to find Sita. At last he had to come back to a hermit called Nart, whom he had met on the way to Lanka, and Nart gave the proper direction of the garden where Sita was kept as a prisoner.

Next evening he met Sita, sad and forlorn. Sita was going to hang herself just when Hanuman found her. Hanuman showed her the ring and gave Rama's message. Sita wanted Rama to come as soon as possible.

Hanuman wanted to teach Ravana a lesson and give him a taste of what he was capable of. He started uprooting trees and houses and the thousand sons of Ravana came to attack him. Hanuman fought and put them to death. Ravana sent his son Intarachit who used his magic bow to send out arrows of Naga serpents which caught and tied up Hanuman. He was taken to the ten-headed Ravana who tried several methods of execution but they all failed.

Hanuman told Ravana that he could only be killed by fire. Ravana believed him and tied up his long tail with cotton well-soaked in oil and set it alight. The great Hanuman leaped from palace to palace, with the burning tail and soon Lanka City was in flames. He had been told by a hermit that he could put out the fire by his own saliva. After setting the city aflame Hanuman used his own salive, put out the fire and rushed back to Rama.

Ravana had great influence with Indra and requested Indra to rebuild a more beautiful Lanka City, which he did.

Meanwhile, Rama was not too pleased with Hanuman's performance in Lanka. But the war council that Rama convened excused Hanuman. Rama hurriedly marched on and came to Kantakala Hill just opposite Lanka island.

The ocean had to be crossed. Hanuman organised thousands of monkeys and brought mountains of huge boulders, trees and bamboos and started constructing a bridge. Even squirrels helped in carrying earth. Rama patted a squirrel with his three fingers and since then all the squirrels bear three marks on their bodies.

**Ravana's dream**

Ravana had a strange dream. He dreamt that a white vulture came flying from the east and met a black vulture coming from the west. The black vulture was killed in the fight with the white vulture. A demon came out with an oil lamp of coconut shell at the place where the black vulture fell dead. The demon was burnt by the dripping of the oil from the lamp.

Ravana was distressed by this strange dream and asked Bhibek the soothsayer what it meant. Bhibek said that the dream was very ominous. Lanka will be destroyed by the fire which meant Sita. The enemy from the east was Rama, the white vulture who would put Ravana, the black vulture to death along with all his relatives and men.

Bhibek asked Ravana to immediately return Sita to her husband and avoid the fight with Rama. Queen Monto also advised this. Ravana was furious. He said Bhibek was not loyal and turned him out of Lanka; his wife was made a serf and all his properties confiscated. Bhibek went and joined Rama after swearing allegiance.

Hanuman, Sugriva and the thousands of monkeys built large mountains and made the bridge in spite of the hindrances thrown up by Ravana. Rama and the army crossed the bridge and looked for a camping ground in Lanka. Ravana had become desperate and tried to play a trick. He deputed Panurat to entice and lead the army to a cool and shady spot where the army would like to camp. Panurat did it and quickly concealed himself under the earth with the idea that at the proper time he would upturn the whole camp site causing the death of Rama and his large army.

Bhibek was surprised to hear that there was a suitable camp site beyond the Emerald Hills and said that there must be some trick. Rama deputed Hanuman, who immediately found that there was an abundance of ripe fruit on the trees on the camp site but there were no insects.

Hanuman scratched the earth and went down and found Panurat supporting the whole camping site from underneath. Hanuman fought with Panurat and killed him. Immediately on the death of Panurat the land turned into a barren and inhospitable site.

Bhibek pronounced the site near the Emerald Hills to be auspicious. The Emerald Hills were guarded by Kumpasoon and his giants. Hanuman fought Kumpasoon and put him to death along with his giants. Rama and his army then shifted to the site near the Emerald Hills and encamped.

**Ongkot's visit to Ravana**

War also has its rules. Rama did not want to start a fight with Ravana without giving him a chance to make peace.

Ongkot was sent as Rama's ambassador to deliver the message that either Sita be immediately released or there would be a fight. Ongkot forced his entry to Ravana's court. By magic powers he lengthened his tail enormously and made it coil round and round to form a seat and sat on it and made his head on a level with Ravana. Ongkot delivered his message.

Ravana was very angry at the nonchalant attitude of the messenger and ordered him to be caught and executed. But Ongkot was more shrewd. He jumped to the top of the palace and the soldiers that came up to catch him were thrown down and killed. Ongkot made his way to Rama and gave him his report.

Ravana used his magic to put up a huge umbrella that made the whole city of Lanka dark. He thought it would be easy to attack Rama's men in darkness. But when he was asked Sugriva broke the umbrella to pieces.

Ravana sent his brother Kumphakarn to fight Rama. There was a severe fight and Lakshman was badly wounded. Hanuman was sent to get some herbal plants from a distant hill, which he did and Lakshman's life was saved. Rama himself fought with Kumphakarn and Kumphakarn was killed.

**The fight with Intarachit**

Ravana was very perturbed and thought his son Intarachit who had once defeated Indra would be able to put Rama and his men to death. Intarachit was asked to fight Rama. He wanted some time to perform a particular ceremony which would enable his darts to have deadly poison.

Bhibek found out about it due to his celestial knowledge. The ceremony was interrupted and Intarachit faced

Lakshman and injured him, Hanuman and others very badly. Bhibek helped them to get back their consciousness and with magic their lives were saved.

Intarachit again went to the forest to pray to get extra power for his weapons. But the ceremony was again destroyed by Lakshman and Intarachit was deprived of all his magic weapons.

But Intarachit was no coward. He fought a bitter fight with Lakshman and was killed. Ravana was desperate now that he had lost his son. Ravana came out to fight himself. Rama fought him and the fight lasted till dusk came on. Ravana went back to the town.

Ravana deputed his brother Sahasdeja who had a magic truncheon and his nephew Saeng-Atit who also had a magic lens which would burn up whatever it turned towards. But Hanuman killed Sahasdeja and Saeng-Atit was killed in the battle by Rama and Lakshman.

Thus the battle went on in turn. Ravana was being advised by some of his friends and well-wishers to return Sita to Rama. His grandfather Maleevaraj who resided at the top of a hill in heaven also asked him to give back Sita and end the fight. But Ravana would not listen to him.

Ravana's body was cut by Rama several times but Ravana would not die. His soul was not in the body but secreted elsewhere. Bhibek told Rama that Ravana's soul was kept in a case strongly guarded by Kobut, the hermit teacher of Ravana and that his soul had to be destroyed at the same time as his body.

Hanuman was deputed and somehow he managed to take it away from the hermit, and substituted an imitation case where the soul was kept. Hanuman played a trick on the hermit. He told the hermit he had deserted Rama and wanted to join Ravana and appealed to the hermit to take him to Ravana. The simple hermit teacher of

Ravana was taken in by the ruse and presented Hanuman to Ravana. Hanuman abused Rama mercilessly and Ravana was convinced that Hanuman had deserted Rama.

Ravana made Hanuman the heir-apparent to the throne of Lanka and sent him to fight Lakshman the next day. Hanuman put up the show so well that even his monkey-allies took him as a renegade. Ravana was very pleased at this.

Next day the fight was resumed and Ongkot who had been entrusted with the case containing Ravana's soul brought the case to Hanuman who showed it to Ravana. Ravana then realised that his time was up. He bade farewell to his wife and his friendly giants and boldly faced Rama for a fight.

Great was the last fight: an arrow of Rama's pierced Ravana and simultaneously Hanuman took out the soul from the case and crushed it. Ravana, the powerful king of the giants fell down dead. Bhibek, Ravana's wife Nang Monto and the others wept bitterly.

Sita asked Rama to invite all the gods to gather and to put her to the ordeal by fire to test if she had kept herself chaste and clean all these fourteen years she was a captive at Ravana's palace. This was done. Palee made up a huge fire. Sita walked through the fire and with every step the fire was changed into a lotus. Rama took her arm and made her sit by his side.

Rama gave the throne of Lanka to Bhibek. Rama returned to Ayudhya and was crowned king. Barata and Satru were very happy. Hanuman was made the king of Nopburi but he preferred to be a hermit in the forest at Khao Mondop Hills.

Rama and Sita lived happily for some time at Ayudhya. But a wicked giantess Adula, a relative of Ravana's made a plan. She disguised herself as one of Sita's maids and

remained in Rama's palace. One day when Rama had
gone out to a forest on a pleasure trip, Adula cleverly
coaxed Sita to draw on a slate how Ravana looked. Sita
did not see through the trick and innocently drew the
picture.

Just at that moment Rama returned and was very angry
thinking Sita still thought of Ravana. Adula had disappeared. Rama banished Sita at once and asked
Lakshman to execute her.

Lakshman did not have the heart to carry out Rama's
instructions. He left Sita in the forest and took back the
heart of a dead deer and showed it to Rama.

Sita found shelter in the hermitage of the sage Vajmarika. She was pregnant when she was left in the forest. She bore a son. She left the baby son at the hermit's cave and went out in the forest to collect fruits, herbs and leaves. One day the hermit got up from his meditation and found the baby boy gone. He was perturbed. He made a fire ceremony and created another baby boy exactly like Sita's child.

Just then Sita returned with the baby boy whom she had taken to the river for a bath. Sita reared both the baby boys and called them Mongkut and Lob. The hermit trained the boys in archery and other arts.

Once the royal horse was let loose. The idea was that the royal horse should not be made captive unless the captor wanted to fight the king. The two boys in the hermitage caught the horse. Hanuman went to release the horse and fight the captor. The two children beat Hanuman to unconsciousness, tied him up and put an enchantment round him so that none but his master could untie him. When Hanuman got back his consciousness he found he could not untie himself. He sent a message to Rama who deputed Satru and Barata to get the captors. There was a long fight and Mongkut was captured and taken to Rama but Lob escaped to his mother Sita.

Sita gave him a magic ring from her finger and said the ring could break any fetters. Lob went to Rama's palace and managed to send a jug of water to Mongkut and put the ring into the jug. The water was taken by a beautiful damsel Rompa who wanted to help Lob. She was allowed to take the water to quench Mongkut's thirst. The guards were charmed with her beauty. As soon as Mongkut saw the ring he recognised it and put it on. The fetters round him fell off. He joined his brother.

Rama was very angry at the escape of Mongkut and led an army to catch the brothers. Father and sons fought but none could defeat the other. Surprised at the valour and fighting skill Rama asked them who they were and he was more surprised when they replied that they were the sons of Sita and had been brought up by a hermit but they had no father. Rama questioned Lakshman and Lakshman confessed he had not executed Sita but had left her in the forest.

Rama approached Sita and wanted her back with the sons. But Sita refused to be reconciled. Rama wanted to commit suicide out of desperation. Sita was in a fix but agreed that the two sons could go with Rama but she would not go. Rama brought back the two sons.

Rama was anxious to get back Sita. He thought of a trick. He had it publicised that Rama was dead and all the court people and women were in mourning. On hearing this Sita came to pay her respects to the body of Rama. She found she had been tricked. Rama and his people surrounded her and would not let her go. Sita beseeched the help of the gods and Mother Earth split open. Sita went down to the underground and the king of the serpents Phya Virun-Nagaraja received her.

In the end the God Indra and the creator Shiva brought about a reconciliation and Sita could not disobey the creator. Rama went back to Ayudhya with Sita and lived there happily.*

*The story of Ramayana known as Ramakian is extremely popular and every child in Thailand knows some of the stories. In fact, Thai culture is very much based on the Ramayana; the folklore and the folk arts are actively associated with it.

The Ramakian version in Thailand is, however, not an adaptation of Valmiki's Ramayana which is prevalent in North India. It is more after the Tamil version which again is largely drawn from the Jaini Ramayana of the great Jain scholar Hem Chandra. The Ramakian highlights Ravana, Hanuman and the giants. The story has been depicted in frescoes on the walls of the Temple of the Emerald Buddha in the Grand Palace of Bangkok. Khon mask dance has evolved out of the dramatisation of the Ramakian.

King Rama I wrote a version of the Ramakian and M.L. Manich Jumsai, M.A. (Cantab) has translated it. The version presented here is adapted from that book.